Europe: Faith and Plan

Oswald Mosley

Europe: Faith and Plan

Oswald Mosley

ISBN-13: 978-1-913176-04-4

Sanctuary Press Ltd
71-75 Shelton Street
Covent Garden
London
WC2H 9JQ

www.sanctuarypress.com
Email: info@sanctuarypress.com

Contents

Contents

Introduction

THE object of this book is to suggest that the complete Union of Europe with an European Government is now a necessity.

Both the arrangements made by the six countries for the gradual introduction of a common market, and the even slower and more hesitant methods proposed by the government of Britain, will prove completely inadequate in face of the economic crises of the next few years. Nothing but European Government can move with the decision and speed which are now necessary.

Nothing but the decisive act of making an European Government can overcome the multitude of small interests and minor problems, which impede present efforts. We must plunge into the water and start swimming, if we are ever to get anywhere. This is the whole effective theme of this book, and the reasons for this view are argued in some detail. It is a plea for the union of all who believe in this one decisive act of making an European Government, in disregard of all other differences which could be discussed later and determined at European elections.

At the same time the book does suggest a comprehensive policy for the new Europe, in practically all the main questions of the day. In particular, an economic method is proposed whereby an entirely free system, in a large and viable area such as Europe-Africa, could solve the recurrent crises of the present European countries, by an economic leadership of Government which could secure greater results than the communist system, without the compulsion of soviet tyranny. The method proposed is described as the wage-price mechanism, and it is argued that Government can do all that is necessary by a system of continuous action at this key point and by certain related measures, while otherwise allowing and encouraging a much greater freedom than prevails today.

The book is primarily addressed to the European problem, but it is clear that if such an European wage policy were effective, it could operate equally as an American wage policy in meeting the economic problem of that country; the same method could be used in any area large enough to contain its own foodstuffs and raw materials, and to enable the organisation of its own market.

The familiar objection that this kind of thinking is too far ahead, and is more appropriate to the next century than the present day, is likely in some respects to be raised again on this occasion. The short answer is surely that we have suffered enough from thinking behind events, and that it might now be an advantage to try to think ahead of them. In any case, events are now moving so fast in this new age of science, that what is far ahead today can easily become out-dated tomorrow. The coming economic crises will compel entirely fresh thinking, and the reasons for believing them sooner or later to be inevitable are summarised in this book.

If we delay action until the full rigour of the major economic crisis is upon us, nothing will meet the situation except the full rigour of a siege economy. All the divided nations of Europe will then be fighting for survival, and nothing except the strongest measures will secure survival. No one can desire such a situation and such measures; it is a purpose of this book to argue that timely action can still avert both. It is better to enter Europe before than after a disaster.

All the matters of detailed economic policy here discussed, the proposals for a practical settlement between East and West, the idea for a modern structure of government in a new scientific epoch, and various thoughts on many other problems, are suggestions for consideration, for acceptance in whole or in part, or for rejection. None of them affects intrinsically the main theme, which is an argument for the immediate creation of an European Government. To agree about that, does not oblige agreement about anything else; and certainly not agreement with me.

Should not those who feel alike about this one impelling need of European Government, come together and set aside all lesser things? The need is too big to be impeded and frustrated by any difference on other matters, past or present. There will be plenty of time for other arguments, and also for much more thinking, when Europe is made. If this book can persuade some in favour of this one decisive act, a work is done.

Chapter 1

Europe Divided

THIS book is a statement of faith in Europe and a short outline of the policy suggested to make real that belief. I first gave precise expression to my feelings on the matter with the words Europe a Nation in 1948, and even in 1937 attempted, with an essay called The World Alternative, to persuade the divided Europeans in favour of a practical and natural union and against the crime and folly of another fratricidal war. There is, of course, nothing new in the idea of a United Europe, which has been ardently desired by thinkers and men of action from every European country since the time of Charlemagne. Europeans of vision and spirit have always wanted it. The only new factor is that now it is a necessity. Modern science, industrial technique and also, unfortunately, new weapons compel it in a shrinking world. The fairest and brightest prospects of a higher form of life recommend it, while darkness threatens if this natural centre and balance of the world, which is Europe, lies much longer broken, splintered, divided and helpless.

It is the strangest event of history that nearly 300 million people of such outstanding gifts and such great achievements should now be in this position. Europe has become accustomed to being the dependent of America as the only alternative to being the victim of Russia. Yet any newcomer to the scene would surely think it as ridiculous as it is tragic. Certainly any great figure from Europe's past would so regard it; the situation would seem to him unbelievable. And if we look at the matter objectively, the whole business is so mad that it would appear incredible.

The population of Europe is more numerous than that of either Russia or America. The science and technical skill of our people is in no way inferior to that of America, and was far greater than that of Russia until that country devoted a much higher proportion of its total wealth than any other nation to the production of scientists and technicians, at the expense of general education and consumption, while we played the fool by dissipating our far greater productive potential in the smoke of every conceivable folly. The reserves of energy in our Europeans is at least as great as the energy of Russia or America; if we had put a fraction of the effort into bringing together a new system which we put into fighting each other, we should long ago have out-stripped them both. Our roots are deeper, our culture is longer, our traditions and way of life are more strongly established, and therefore our stability is greater.

Can it be denied that we are larger in numbers, at least the equal in science and technique, at least the equal in energy, and possibly firmer in character because we have lived longer and done more? And if so, can anyone explain with clear reason why we should cling to America and shiver in fear of Russia, without ever a serious thought of exerting the giant strength of Europe, first to restore the balance of the world and then to lead it to a new level of security and happiness? In fact, there is no reason. Europe is the victim of a complex of past bitterness which is now entirely irrational, but is very useful to those who seek for their own purposes to keep us divided.

The failure of Europe is quite simply a failure of will and spirit. There is no physical impediment, no limitation of nature or of knowledge which prevents the Union of Europe and the rapid development of the highest civilisation this world has yet seen. These countries lie in a geographical unity which modern transport can develop into an economic unity far more complete and integrated than the economy of any individual nation a century ago. They contain within their own borders, or in their adjacent overseas territories, every possible foodstuff and raw material which man or industry can require. It is universally admitted that modern mass production methods would naturally and speedily develop in response to such a market, and that the consequent increase in distributable wealth would greatly raise the standard of life. It could also provide a surplus of resources for scientific research and development which could both assure the future and greatly accelerate the whole process of human evolution.

The advantages are so obvious that they cannot seriously be denied. There is no physical reason why the decision should not be taken immediately to set all these saving and beneficent forces in motion, with sure and early results in the solution or substantial improvement of most present dangers and difficulties. The motives which inhibit the Union of Europe are entirely psychological. They should be examined calmly and seriously by all who are concerned with the present situation, for objective reasoning alone can cure them. There is no limitation of material circumstance. This is a failure of the will, a weakness of the spirit.

The emotions which inhibit the will to necessary change are by no means all unworthy. A mistaken sense of patriotism is partly responsible; mistaken, because true patriotism is living, organic, developing and forward-looking, not dying and nostalgic for an irretrievable past. A type of conservatism which is in itself healthy and desirable erects another barrier to the progress without which nothing can be finally conserved. It is a sound instinct to conserve traditions, institutions, an outlook and a way of life which are deep-rooted and therefore confer the supreme benefit of stability on the society they sustain. But in an age of rapid change they must be capable of quick adaptation to fresh facts and of swift development to meet new situations, or they become a curse to the community which they have previously blessed.

National feeling is all to the good when it comprises these qualities. No one should seek to destroy them when entering the larger life which is now necessary, only to extend them and give a broader and firmer base to their continued existence. An extension of patriotism is now desirable, not the extinction of that great sentiment.

We must now try to combine the principles of progress and stability which the warfare of political parties has thrown into unnecessary and illogical conflict. For, in reality, continual progress brings chaos without the accompanying principle of stability; and without the progress which responds to new discovery and fresh circumstance, the stability of no society can endure because it becomes opposed to the course of nature and of life. Therefore it is most desirable to preserve the deep-rooted traditions of each present national existence when entering the wider harmony of European Union. But it is fatal to let tradition become unreasoning prejudice which thwarts a natural and essential development. This can only occur when tradition is no longer vital, organic and living, but dead, petrified or in process of decomposition. Opposition to new life does not indicate a healthy regard for the past, but rather the inner decay which precedes collapse.

It is normal for great peoples to fear an immediate loss of national identity when they merge with other peoples in a greater nationhood and life. But in fact it does not occur. This is merely a continuance of a natural process which can be traced in all human evolution, and we are therefore able to observe the true facts from past examples. Throughout history small communities have tended to merge in larger civilisations. In our English case it is not so long ago in terms of history since village fought village until their struggle was merged into the conflict of the Saxon kingdoms, and finally was resolved in the greater wars between England and Wales, and England and Scotland, which preceded the union of Great Britain.

At each stage, no doubt, local patriotism feared extinction, and after long periods it was, of course, true that the former combatants renewed their life and widened their consciousness by some mingling of their blood and of their ideas. But the fear that a political and economic union leads at once to the loss of cultural and national identity is very easily disproved from relatively recent experience. The Scot feels no less Scottish since he was united with the English in Great Britain, the Bavarian felt no less Bavarian when he was united with Prussia in a united Germany, while within France, Italy, Spain and in all the great countries of Europe it is still possible to find people so tenacious of local traditions, custom and outlook that they can scarcely understand each others' language, and regard everyone outside their own locality as a foreigner.

In fact, the integration of existing European nations is only becoming slowly complete by means of radio, newspapers and all the manifold means of modern education. The real fear in human affairs is not so much that the past will be forgotten too soon, as that it will be remembered too long. For the past becomes the enemy of the future when it is exaggerated to the point of making everyone an enemy outside a small domestic circle. We live in an age which requires in mankind a wider, and also a deeper consciousness. Science is moving far faster than the mind and psychology of men. The danger is not that we shall lose too quickly our old selves, but that we shall not find quickly enough the developed mind and character necessary to a new environment.

It is not, therefore, difficult to understand why our policy "Europe a Nation" encounters so much opposition. We propose nothing less than the complete Union of Europe as an integral nation. Europe a Nation means that Europe should become a nation in the same full sense that Britain, Germany, France, Italy and Spain are nations today. The main object of this book is to prove that nothing less can meet the case. No wonder that all the forces of lethargy, old custom and vested interests are ranged against it until increasing stress makes plain the necessity.

Even the very limited steps towards European integration taken by present governments have met such resistance. So far they have done little more than I proposed before the war. The countries involved have not merged their essential sovereignties, they have simply begun to make a bloc of European powers with certain common economic arrangements. The dividing line between them and us is clear in my present proposal. We believe it is now necessary to make a European nation with a European Government, a complete merging of present national sovereignties in a unified European state. The division of principle is at least clear.

It is natural to regard our position as extreme until the reasons which have led to it are examined in more detail. But at present we are only discussing the feeling against any move, however limited, toward European integration, and the underlying psychology which gives it a natural force. In fact the sentiment against a complete union is unlikely to be any stronger than the resistance which now retards a partial union, particularly when it can be clearly explained that popular and valuable institutions like the British Crown need be in no way affected, and that culture, literature and language, so far from being impaired, will find a wider sphere and a deeper significance and appreciation.

When necessity makes it plain that union must come, plain sense will indicate that it is better to have a union complete and effective than a union partial and limited enough to fail. The sentiment against action is always present, it is often less strong against great action than small measures. And in any case we shall not get this thing through until it is clearly necessary; that is why we have not had it before. It was not enough for far-seeing men to desire it; vision and passion for a higher level of life were inadequate, as so often in human affairs, until the harsh reinforcement of necessity. Europe has waited many centuries for the proof of this deep need. Events will soon provide it.

Great changes of this kind have usually come in the past through wars. Fortunately this means is excluded in a modern world which retains any degree of sanity - the condition on which all life now depends - because the new weapons of science have become so deadly that one system cannot by war be imposed on another but only universal death on all mankind. It is rather the failure of an economic system, either by reason of internal disintegration or by force of the rivalry and competition of a stronger system, which is now likely to bring decisive changes.

Such failure of the existing economic system in Western Europe can lead to beneficent change in a decision to unite Europe and to make a new and viable system. On the other hand it can be a disaster if a mood of despair leads to the victory of communism. It is plainly, therefore, in the interests of all the diverse enemies of Europe on the one hand to discourage the will to European Union, and on the other to emphasise in all possible ways the rival attractions of communism. For this task they are, of course, powerfully aided by all the nationalist, conservative forces of inertia which we have already discussed, and also by every tendency of contemporary decadence which always prefers the passive acceptance of vigour from somebody else to the positive exertion of creative vitality. Both these forces are today unconsciously inhibiting the Union of Europe and promoting the victory of communism. Far more conscious forces are, of course, very actively concerned to produce the same result. Their purpose is to paralyse the European will. For in present circumstances this great deed must be an act of will.

The interest of communism in promoting the division of Europe is obvious. But it is equally clear that such overt efforts would not have much effect if they were not assisted on this occasion by all the normal forces of inertia and decline. People like to continue doing what they are accustomed to do, as long as they possibly can. They hate change so much that they will seldom move out of the old house until it falls about their ears. An earthquake is usually needed to shift them, and, as this convulsion of war is now happily absent, the inner rot can go so far without anybody noticing anything in particular that the final collapse can be very rapid and extremely dangerous.

It is indeed curious to observe people with nothing whatever to gain personally from the victory of communism, resisting by every possible means the changes which are necessary to avert it. Malevolence could not win without this alliance with stupidity. Communism can never come to Europe without the powerful assistance it derives from the natural conservatism of the European peoples.

The strong resistance of many great vested interests to all necessary changes often creates the suspicion of some collusion between the money power and communism. And in some cases, undoubtedly, the more international elements of the financial world have taken a gamble on communism. But in the great majority of cases it is not sympathy with communism but a natural antipathy to change which makes such men the unconscious allies of the forces of destruction. Even when it can be proved that they stand to gain far more in the constructive task of building a European-African economy, which would provide far more wealth for all to share, they much prefer to draw the diminishing rewards of a system which is failing before their eyes, but is hallowed by custom and gilded by memories of the old easy life. Few men are wicked but the great majority are lazy. And laziness, as we all know, seeks every excuse for putting off the hour of action. Those who are interested in preventing the action which now alone can save the European peoples, have therefore an easy task in providing the great excuse for laziness by pretending that all is well, when it is clear that much is very wrong. When they can add past bitterness to present laziness, their victory is almost complete.

The resentments of the first World War vanished with remarkable speed, particularly when we consider that the casualties of the Western European peoples were far heavier in the first war than the second, and the effects in most individual homes were therefore far harsher. Yet apart from the professional hatred of one or two journals a real goodwill between the peoples soon returned. The war was forgotten, and became something that few wanted to remember. Now, more than a decade after the Second War, no one is allowed to forget it for a moment. Every instrument of propaganda is continually in action to remind everyone of its worst features.

Europe Divided

Can a week go by for any reader of newspapers, radio listener and viewer, or cinema goer, when he does not read, hear or see something which is well calculated to stir up his most bitter feelings against another European people, and could any process be better calculated to prevent or delay European Union? It is true that a morbid preoccupation with horror and atrocity is both a phenomenon of this epoch and a usual symptom of social decadence. But does not this curiosity itself derive largely from the atrocity propaganda which accompanied and followed the war? And what interest can it have, except to make people hate one another? The atrocity business lies at the very root of European divisions. It is the psychological basis of the whole attack on the future life and well-being of the European peoples. From the outset it must be met, and fearlessly, relentlessly examined. The story that some nations have a "double dose of original sin" - the derisive phrase of Mr. Gladstone, when rebutting attacks upon the Irish - must be exposed as the tragic absurdity which it is.

There should be no such thing as particularly liking or particularly disliking some particular people within the family of Europe. An adult European of balanced mind, who possesses the main languages, knows perfectly well that the rational attitude is to like some Englishmen, Frenchmen, Germans, Italians, Spaniards, etc., and to dislike other Englishmen, Frenchmen, Germans, Italians, Spaniards, etc. This attitude is rational because some in each great country have similar values, views, outlooks and tastes to ourselves which make them sympathetic to us, and others in each great country have opposite qualities which make then antipathetic. It is a sure sign of stupidity, narrowness and general inadequacy, a sad limitation of intellect and character, to generalise in like or dislike of some particular people. Directly a man has grown beyond the most childish inhibitions he finds that his sympathies are determined more by natural affinities than by geographical boundaries; the division is of the soul rather than the soil.

This is certainly as true within the family of Europe as in the family of daily experience. We may reasonably dislike an aunt and like an uncle, or vice versa, but not regard the neighbouring cousins as malevolent insects from an alien planet. These ridiculous and tragic anachronisms are kept alive by memories of fratricidal wars, by restricted education, by lack of travel facilities and, above all, by the continuous and malevolent propaganda of powerful forces which have a vested interest in keeping Europeans apart. The peoples are subjected to a continual flood of atrocity propaganda.

I approach this question with a long and consistent record of opposing bullying of all kinds. The ill-treatment of the powerless or weak has always seemed to me to be the most despicable of vices and I have given effect to this view in repeated battles against various bullies throughout my political life. I was still the youngest member of the British Parliament when I became involved in the first great row of my political career through opposing the systematic shooting of a defenceless crowd which was incapable of escape at Amritsar, India. After that, still as the youngest M.P., I began with a handful of other members the long Parliamentary battle against the atrocious methods used for the suppression of the Irish people by the Black and Tans, a struggle which culminated in the Irish Treaty. Throughout my political life I defy anyone to find a single occasion on which I have supported bullying; my attitude in such matters has invariably been against the bully and for the oppressed.

The ridiculous charge was made against me before the war that I used violent and brutal methods to throw out of my meetings those who came with organised violence to break them up. That subject has been dealt with elsewhere in a book compiled by some of my friends with a wealth of detailed, rebutting evidence which I will not here repeat. The broad facts are known to nearly all British people who were adult at that time. Meetings had been broken up all over Britain for years before I even began, if they were regarded with disfavour by organised bands of red roughs.

The answer of the old parties had been to close down public meetings, and to rely on selected and ticketed meetings of their supporters and on the great newspapers whose assistance they could always command. We were a new movement which had no Press and had to gain supporters at meetings for which the public paid by buying their seats or contributing to collections. The public meeting was our only available method, and we had to defend our meetings or close down. I, therefore, led and organised young men who were prepared to throw out of our meetings, with their bare hands, the armed roughs who came to break them up and to prevent British audiences listening to the speech they had come to hear. The result was that the largest public meetings ever assembled in Britain were held, without exception, in complete peace and order throughout the last three years before the war. If that record be brutality, I plead guilty. If not, no single case can be suggested against me in which I have not stood for the oppressed and against the oppressor.

This digression at least serves to establish my personal record with regard to what are loosely termed atrocities. My only first-hand knowledge is concerned with the comparatively mild version of being held for three and a half years in British prisons (without trial or possibility of charge, because we had committed no offence), while some eight hundred of my principal colleagues were detained in British concentration camps on the Isle of Man. It was explained that the object of the exercise was to prevent us from persuading the British people to make peace during a war fought to preserve the basic freedoms. Having always opposed imprisonment without trial, on the grounds that it was a symptom of incompetence in a government to be unable to frame adequate laws and persuade the people to accept them, as well as a manifest injustice, I reject this method both as a long-standing opponent and as a relatively recent victim.

My every instinct and preconception is against such procedure, and still more against the covertly organised bullying, the cowardly tyranny of the loutish gaoler over a defenceless prisoner, the sly sadism of the minority of habitual perverts who get the chance at such moments to satisfy in particular the general demand of an ignoble epoch for revenge. It cannot too often be repeated that revenge is the hallmark of small minds. These things might not have happened if choleric old gentlemen and well-stuffed old ladies had not created the necessary atmosphere in the foetid hatreds of their country dugouts.

All nations possess such people. Most war crimes are only a question of necessity, opportunity and degree. The sense of necessity arises more easily in the fury of defeat, opportunity for the bestial minority in all peoples occurs more easily in the chaos of a disintegrating society, and the degree is greater in such conditions because it is easier to do more horrible things than usual without being noticed. If we have to assess or compare guilt it is surely a question of condition rather than degree.

In any moral judgment the man who commits a few crimes without any shadow of excuse in necessity or passion is more guilty than the man who commits many crimes in the hot blood of war. It is a difference recognised by most law, the difference between a calculating poisoner and a violent homicide. If we are driven to compare the crimes of nations, much could be said in this respect. Crimes committed in the agony of defeat, at the end of a great war, might even appear less reprehensible under impartial examination than methods used subsequently in time of peace to obtain evidence concerning those crimes. But it is surely enough to cleanse the air of Europe for us all to admit that all are in some degree guilty, that in this matter there is no immaculate state. The best that anyone can claim is that he is less bad than the rest, and he would be better engaged in resolving to prevent the recurrence of things that shame us all, events which have been a disgrace to the whole of Europe.

It is a curious thing that the only atrocity stories which are systematically kept alive are those best calculated to keep Europe divided; namely, everything of this kind which was done by any

German in the Second World War. Sometimes it is suggested that these things were proved to be done on the deliberate order of the Government, and on a scale which put them into an altogether different category from anything done elsewhere. When the proofs of Nuremberg are mentioned, the necessary comment is surely that no proof can be finally accepted by history if it comes from courts in which the accuser is also judge and jury in his own case. Before these facts are established beyond doubt, they must be examined afresh in entirely neutral courts, and such a court should be competent to enquire not only into atrocities committed by Germans, but into the shameful deeds of all.

The vexed question of government orders, and the degree of knowledge possessed by leading men concerning what was being done by subordinates, is always most difficult to determine, as those of us know well enough who were engaged in combating the Irish atrocities in the British Parliament. But even if it were true that everything done in German concentration camps was done on the deliberate orders of the government and with full knowledge of all the leaders, how could the German people possibly be held responsible for it? At most only a relatively small handful of men could have had anything at all to do with it, and the mass of the people could not possibly have known anything about it. And even if it were true that the German Government ordered these atrocities in time of war, can anyone contend that they were even comparable in scale or degree with the atrocities which the Russian Government ordered in time of peace, and scarcely even troubled to deny?

Why, then, do we have a continual barrage of propaganda against German atrocities and scarcely a word nowadays about the far greater crimes of the Russians? Is there any explanation except that the first propaganda performs a service to communism, and the second a disservice? To carry the subject a little further back, have the French people been blamed for evermore on account of the atrocities committed during the French Revolution? After all, they occurred frequently in the public squares of large cities, with any number of people looking on and enjoying the spectacle. But, whenever they were not at war, this did not prevent the people of England from using every possible occasion to enjoy the great amenities of French civilisation.

Why then alone of all the tragic incidents of history are certain events in the dark privacy of German concentration camps during the final frenzy of an agonising defeat in a decisive war, used to foster hatred and artificially to maintain the divisions of peoples whom every natural instinct and mutual interest should unite? The answer is, surely, that communism and its conscious and unconscious allies - more sinister in many respects than communism itself, because they are well concealed - have a paramount interest in perpetuating the divisions of Europe, and these interests are at present for various obscure reasons being assiduously served by the incessant propaganda which the dominant money power of the West commands. There is something which is surely very unnatural about this position. Britain fought the French over a far longer period and much more often than the Germans. When national circumstances and interests changed these wars ceased, and the normal Englishman now feels nothing but the warmest affections for the French. In the case of the Germans the national interests which formerly led to a clash (even then only on account of mistaken policies) have now completely disappeared, and have been replaced by complete community of interest in all major questions of the day.

Trade warfare, it is true, will certainly be kept alive so long as we insist on preserving small uneconomic units which are obliged to fight each other on world markets in order to sell enough exports to pay for the food and raw materials which they do not possess in sufficient quantities within their own borders. But the last clash of interests will disappear entirely the moment we decide to make a viable economic unit of Europe-Africa, with no balance of payment problem because it will contain both its own market and source of supply. The struggle of Britain and Germany, either in terms of trade or culture, will then be no more acute than the contest between Yorkshire and Lancashire within present Britain, or between Prussia and Bavaria within present Germany. The two countries will be able to stimulate each other with a friendly and beneficent rivalry in many ways, but they will no longer be able to destroy each other by destructive competition on world markets which deprives one or the other of the means of life. For it requires only a very slight knowledge of elementary arithmetic to observe that everyone cannot in these conditions achieve a favourable balance of payments at the same time.

So we are driven back continually to the question: why, when every natural instinct and mutual interest now indicate union, we should be kept apart by a vicious propaganda of very doubtful truth in the past and with no relevance at all to the present? The long and short of the matter is that every great country not only in the past, but in modern times, has committed atrocities. They may vary in quantity or degree - this can be a matter of long and bitter argument - but all have done it. Not one is innocent in this respect.

I cite the case of atrocities committed by British Government in India and Ireland, of which I had definite knowledge because I collected the evidence to oppose British Government in Parliament. Since then distinguished men in British politics have averred from evidence they have collected and collated that similar things have been done in Cyprus and in Kenya. Also men with famous names in various other countries - in some cases, even since the war - have alleged with the support of definite evidence that their own governments have committed atrocities.

In the light of all Europe's recent history it is disingenuous nonsense to pretend that Germany is the only guilty party. It is more, it is a deliberate lie circulated for the vile purpose of perpetuating the division of Europe and for promoting the ultimate victory of communism. In the meantime it serves also the squalid purpose of those who snatch financial gain from the decay and collapse of a dying system, rather than make the effort to benefit both themselves and all Europe by honestly earning the far greater rewards of constructive tasks in building the new system.

As observed, it is manifestly unfair to blame whole peoples for things which have been done by a small handful in each country. The past has also proved it to be hysterical nonsense to blame a political creed for what happened at its inception. Who today would seek to fasten the blame for all the horrors of the French Revolution, and the bloodshed of the wars of Napoleon, on the English Liberal Party which governed Britain through some of her best years before the first world War; The European liberal movement began in the blood and turmoil of revolution and war, but continued, grew and developed until it became the calm, ordered and beneficent force of the nineteenth century. We could perhaps claim some credit that the most constructive phase of Liberalism began in the British Isles. But it must be admitted that the initial impulse came from the French Revolution, which also provided a striking experience of what to preserve and discard in the liberal creed. Those who come later in a new development have the chance to learn both from the successes and the errors of those who began.

In all nature the pangs of birth are severe, particularly in political nature. No fully grown man should be blamed for the pain or even the blood that accompanied his birth. For the long memory to linger on these things is to create a complex which can be disastrous to the whole psyche of Europe. That is precisely why we are continually invited to think about them.

Things were done in haste and passion which should now be forgotten. All who were drawn to the new movement of European dynamism and renaissance were people in too much of a hurry. It was a fault on the right side, for the results of the succeeding inertia are now plain to see. We felt that something must be done, and done quickly, to release the new and beneficent forces of science and to wipe away unnecessary suffering from the face of humanity. We were impatient with the forces of inertia, reaction and anarchy which opposed the new European order of mind and will that we believed alone could do these things with the speed that was necessary.

Impatience is right in such conditions until it collides with the basic morality which we derive from three thousand years of European history and tradition. Even action to prevent necessary poverty and suffering is too dearly bought if it destroys these values. It is certainly gained at too high a price if it risks fratricidal war. These are the faults of dynamism from which men of action must learn in the future. I myself, though guilty of neither war nor atrocity, was certainly always in too much of a hurry. So let those responsible for the present condition of the world be alone in the sublime assurance that they have committed no mistakes.

The catastrophe of this generation has destroyed the old landmarks of politics, and the modern mind should equally eliminate their memory. We have passed beyond Fascism and beyond many tenets of the old Democracy, because science has rendered them irrelevant in a world which confronts us with new facts. Not only are the facts of the post-war period new, but science is continually adding still newer facts. Old policies have no relevance to the present, and old memories of bitterness should have no place in it either.

One great lesson alone we can all derive from the past. We owe to Europe self-restraint in moments of passion, and kindness at all times to our kindred. These evil things which have occurred are not only wrong, they do not pay. In the end they destroy those who commit them. The time-honoured standards of the European alone can endure. In the events of a great age, honour, truth and manly restraint are not only as necessary as in the past but more than ever essential. The great qualities in man should grow in proportion to the age, not diminish. Let us remember the past only long enough to learn this. Then let us forget. Europe needs a great act of oblivion, before a new birth.

Chapter 2

Europe A Nation

EUROPE a Nation is an idea which anyone can understand. It is simple, but should not on that account be rejected; most decisive, root ideas are simple. Ask any child: what is a nation? He will probably reply, a nation has a government. And, in fact, this is the right answer, for the first thing to note about a nation is that it is a country consisting of a people with their own government. Many deeper reflections naturally follow; questions of geography, race, history, which contributed to the evolution of this fact, a people with a government which is a nation. But the simple, decisive point which defines a nation, is that it has a government. That is why the dividing question of modern Europe is whether or not we desire a European government. It is the purpose of this book to answer, yes. And in the end all will find it necessary to make up their minds on which side of this question they stand.

An idea so clear and so decisive will eventually be supported with a passionate enthusiasm by its adherents, and they will continually gain force as the obscurity, weakness and muddle of the opposing and conflicting opinions produce ever-increasing confusion. Compromise solutions adopted by politicians who do not desire European government, but are driven reluctantly towards the larger way of life by the progressive failure of their small, individual systems, will prove ever more inadequate as events gather momentum. It will appear more and more evident that the complete solution of Europe a Nation alone can meet Europe's problems, and the mounting enthusiasm of the peoples for a clear cut idea which is both urged by necessity and inspired by idealism will finally face everyone with the question, for or against. In the end the only way to get great things done is to do things in a great way. If we meet a vital necessity with a clear decisive idea which everyone can understand and which evokes a high ideal, the people will respond directly they see the necessity, understand the plan, and feel the appeal of a moving cause. That is why in life it is often easier to get great things done than to get small things managed. In a supreme moment, like the wars of the past, the peoples of Europe were capable of every exertion and of every sacrifice. There is now a real need to evoke the same fervent spirit for a decisive act, not of destruction but of construction, for a work not of division and death, but of union and life. This can only be done by an idea which is clear, and an idea which is great. Europe a Nation alone can awaken the vital response of the peoples.

We need the swing and idealism of the people to break through the maze of diplomacy and haggling which today obstructs European union. The statesmen of the divided nations are lost in the detail of their search for small individual advantage, and the whole which alone can serve the real advantage of all is forgotten. Europe will never be made without a decisive act which has the passionate enthusiasm of the peoples behind it, and that act is the making of European government. It is the duty of all who believe in this saving idea to come together in the continuous campaign necessary to arouse popular enthusiasm for the next big development of human society.

The thought and the passion must come from the centre of political thinking. The good sense which is necessary to this purpose is clearly there, in the centre of all European peoples. Every far-seeing industrialist who is concerned with the future supply and market of his industry is beginning to think in terms of Europe. Every level-headed Trade Union leader who is concerned with safeguarding the present standard of his followers from the growing threat of unfair competition in the chaos of world markets, and with progressively raising it to the level which modern science can make possible and his members therefore justly demand, is beginning to realise that his task is impossible within the limits of small individual countries, without supplies on which they can depend and without a market which they can organise by modern methods.

The main sensible movement of the workers asks, with ever growing insistence, why the mass production which modern technique makes possible cannot bring plenty for all; and they can find the answer only in a large and viable economy which can be consciously organised to equate full production and consumption as science continually increases the power to produce. In all countries, the central mass of people with plain sense and clear eyes - the hitherto successful industrialists, the scientists and technicians who have made that success possible, the workers on whose skill and energy the whole process depends - is coming slowly to realise that the present system of small, divided, uneconomic units cannot last, and before long must yield place to a system large enough and strong enough to make possible modern organisation which will consequently, for the first time, enable them to enjoy the full benefit of modern science.

What all await is the decisive idea and collective political leadership from all European countries which is necessary to awaken the driving enthusiasm of the peoples, and to transmute what is now a general feeling into a concentrated will and victorious cause. The sheer inertia which opposes us has already been considered; both Right and Left contribute to that dead weight. Let us first see what chance they have of saving that economic system at all, even on their present standards, if they maintain their existing positions and pursue further their traditional policies. I will then try to present a definite solution, a concrete answer to the dilemma which the present system faces and which, in the end, its rulers will find to be insurmountable.

We will consider the position of Great Britain in particular, not merely because the author is English but because this country presents among the European nations the most extreme, and therefore the best, example of the fatally difficult position of small, individual, divided nations in a world of economic units so large and powerful as America and Russia. The position of Britain is the most precarious because it is more dependent than any other country on the markets and supplies of the outside world. Britain must sell a larger proportion of total production than any other country in open competition on world markets, in order to purchase the food and raw materials which it lacks within its own boundaries. The full rigours of this position were mitigated in the past by the possession of a colonial Empire, but the present generation has been in haste to discard this screen from the chill wind of competition. So Britain today is undoubtedly in the most exposed position.

Germany comes next among the European nations in order of dependence on world markets; for the result of the war has been to make Germany in economic terms another England, and consequently Great Britain's most severe trade competitor. France comes last in the order of fundamental economic difficulty; for it is a curious paradox of the period that France has naturally, perhaps, the strongest economic position in the world; being blessed by a particularly rich soil, most favourable variations of climate, and a highly skilled and intelligent population. Always tending to be under - rather than over - populated, France has now the opportunity to become entirely self-supporting owing to the discovery of oil deposits and other primary riches in the region of the Sahara.

The great strength of the French economic position offers a paradox on account of a perennial financial disorder which derives from continually unbalanced budgets. The normal troubles of France are not economic but fiscal, and the basis of the economy is so inherently strong that it has endured even the continual inflation which fiscal chaos brings. If France could be persuaded to accept the co-operation of other Europeans in developing some of its natural riches within a system sound and stable enough to command the confidence of the majority of Frenchmen, the standard of life in that country could be rapidly raised to a level which would now seem incredible. This in turn depends on other people looking at the problem as Europeans, and not as the jealous nationals of other states; for instance, regarding the Sahara oil and other African resources as a national European treasure which can possibly solve the most difficult supply questions of the whole Continent.

France has much to gain from the union of Europe in securing the full co-operation which is necessary to the development of her latent wealth. Italy on the other hand has perhaps the most to gain in finding an outlet for the energy and ability of a vital people which today is confined in too small a space; an outlet which would give her access to the overseas wealth of Europe, and an equal partnership in its development and enjoyment.

But we must first consider the facts of the present situation, which threaten in varying degree all the economies of the divided European peoples with destruction. For this purpose we can take Britain as an extreme example of vulnerability to factors which menace not only all European countries but most other small and advanced nations. Britain is most exposed to adverse movements on world markets, precisely because it was the first industrial nation. In the beginning of the industrial revolution she sent manufactured goods all over the world, and received foodstuffs and raw materials in exchange. A habit of trade and a structure of industry were created which rested on selling everywhere, and buying anywhere certain essentials at the cheapest rates available. An immense export trade was the result, with a great volume of imports at a very low price in exchange. Many people became very rich (largely at the expense of the poor who were drawn from the countryside into industrial slums, but we are here studying the cause of the coming economic collapse and not writing a social history) and the great vested interest in that form of life was created.

The original paradise of wealth was, of course, soon affected when other nations became industrialised and severe competition began. Even before the first World War, Britain was feeling the precarious position of a top-heavy industrial structure dependent on export trade to world markets, which by very reason of its exaggerated initial success had destroyed the sound agricultural base, and with it the whole equilibrium of the economy, through the import of food and primary goods far more cheaply than they could be produced at home. This process was intensified when many of these goods became imported without any corresponding export at all, because they represented interest on past loans which were accumulated abroad by the excess of Britain's exports over any immediately necessary imports. The result of it all was the development of a population far bigger than the British Isles could support, and consequently the most extremely vulnerable economic system in the world.

But all the new industrial nations suffered in varying degree from the same chronic disequilibrium. All were exporting to world markets in order to purchase foodstuffs and raw materials which they either could not produce at home, or were disinclined to produce because the exchange of manufactures with primary products gave a higher standard of life. The only two exceptions to the universal vulnerability of industrial nations were first America, which was so large that nearly all foodstuffs and raw materials were contained within its own borders, and later Russia, whose tardy industrial development was equally blessed by the same natural immunity from the struggle for outside markets and supplies. All the others were dependent for their very life on the battle for success in export markets, and it soon became plain that they could not all succeed. For the holy mystery of a favourable balance of payments rests on the simple capacity to sell more than you buy, and it is not difficult to see that everyone cannot do it at the same time. To such basic simplicities can many present complexities and perplexities be reduced, and on such basic fallacies rests the precarious structure of the present system. In normal conditions some must always go under. Consequently, abnormal conditions have long since become necessary to make things work at all.

In our time we have had the two wars of 1914 and 1939, and the two armament booms of the thirties and the fifties, the first in preparation to fight the World War of 1939 and the second in preparation to fight our allies in that war. The moment any thing approaching normal conditions recur, as in the late nineteen twenties, overproduction in relation to the available market invariably begins, with consequent slump and widespread unemployment. In that period a solution was temporarily found by the armament boom of the thirties and the second World War. In the fifties overproduction is threatening again despite the new armament boom, because modern productive power is so great that even with aid of the armament consumption and of all the free gifts showered by America on backward peoples in the political struggle, the present system can find no means whatever to provide an adequate market; in other words it can devise no means for the people to consume what the people produce.

The classic escape into war is closed, since war became more dangerous for politicians than for soldiers. The peaceful means to solve this dilemma without the whole world falling victim to the Marxian-inspired dictatorship of communism will be considered in the next chapter. For the moment we are trying to describe the facts which now face us, and which pose the vital question whether the present system can last another fifteen years while the first part of a new system is created. Some may think the terms of this description are an over-simplification, but most basic truths can be reduced to simplicity; and, in any case, this attempt to clarify and simplify is surely preferable to the deliberate obfuscation with which current mumbo jumbo obscures a situation which baffles it, in the absence of the necessary clarity, decision and character to attempt the discovery and application of a solution.

After the war the economy of the West was maintained by a combination of armament boom, world charity organised from America on an unprecedented scale, and the monetary technique of Maynard Keynes, applied with considerable skill by the Federal Reserve Board of America. The first factor may now be modified by the tardy idea occurring to the Russians that it is better to let the Marxian laws concerning the "internal contradictions of capitalism" take their course, rather than to bolster up the economy of the chief opponent with a continuous armament boom maintained by Soviet menace of a world war, which any sane man must now know would bring the destruction of the communist world at least as surely and completely as that of the capitalist world. The second may equally be qualified by a growing indisposition of the American taxpayer to support the burden of a once prostrate but now largely free living Western Europe, and of Eastern dependencies whose chief symptom of returning vigour has been a most vicious biting of the hand that feeds. In fact, the advent of hard sense in these diverse spheres to both Russia and America has been evinced both in various Soviet attempts to relax tension and in the various attempts of Congress to prune expenditure. So we may soon be left with nothing but the colossus of Keynes to hold up the economy of Western capitalism. An old argument will then be settled; is Keynes enough? Those who at the time answered, no, believe they can now see the beginning of the proof.

Ever since the war the fragile economies of the Western European countries have been sheltered from every natural wind by a quite unusual and inevitably temporary combination of exceptionally favourable circumstances. The long lag in demand which followed an extremely protracted and destructive war was aided by the artificial demand of new small wars all over the place, and by a general condition of world tension which canalised the surplus of American production in the direction of armaments and the mass bribery of populations whose political allegiance it was desired to win. So the real competitive power of America was virtually excluded from world markets.

Now America will soon have to pile up redundant armaments in a world which already possesses more than adequate means to destroy itself, and will also have to give away so large a proportion of total production that it will appear charity on an insane scale to the American masses who thus toil for the enjoyment of ungrateful foreigners. Otherwise America will again be confronted with a problem it has never yet been able to solve: how to enable its own people to consume what its own people can produce, the classic Marxian dilemma stated with un-Marxian simplicity. On present form it appears probable that American surplus production will at that point wash in a devastating flood into the markets of the world, and it also seems likely that this point is not far ahead.

The assumption of recent years has been that the world has passed permanently from the over-production phase of the thirties to the over-consumption condition of the fifties. That view is beginning to prove quite unwarranted, and the reasons for the post-war break in the normal tendency of the capitalist world to over-produce in relation to the available market can now be clearly observed. Not only was the destruction of the last war particularly great and the time lag of recovery longer than usual, not only was the production, the competitive potential of America happily preoccupied with reconstruction and charity, and unhappily, also, with rearmament, but two of the main competitors for world markets were during a long period almost completely eliminated. The first effects of the return of Germany and Japan have now been felt for some time past.

Japan is only the most effective example of a tendency which is proving increasingly fatal to Western industries. Long ago Western finance began to equip the East with modern, rationalised machinery by which unskilled labour in many industries could perform the simplified tasks of mass production as well as white labour, and in some cases better because Orientals endure monotony more easily. Britain led in exporting her machinery and industrial technique to the East, and is now becoming the first victim of a situation which brought larger profits to those who financed the process than the re-equipment of obsolete British industries in the land which so long afforded them not only hospitality but the surplus production which made possible these foreign loans.

So the British workers who produced the exported capital goods, and were thus persuaded to do without a substantial proportion of the wealth they created, now find themselves faced with the deadly competition of coolie labour working the same machines at a fraction of British wages to undercut British industry on all markets. And that process is not diminishing, but is increasing daily. India and all the "liberated" colonies are forming a long queue to demand payment of the sterling balances, which will be used for further industrial equipment for primitive peoples, and another increase of competition from cheap goods on world markets.

In some cases, these balances were accumulated by selling to Britain goods at considerable prices for what was termed a common war effort. In other cases they represented primary products taken over by British Government and sold for very useful dollars. The proceeds of the latter transaction contributed directly or indirectly to the maintenance of the Welfare State during years when Britain was running a trading deficit. But whatever the origin of the sterling balances, the present economic effects of the repayment are plain; Britain must exert herself to send capital goods abroad without any corresponding import, and the only final result of the effort will be a greatly intensified cheap competition against her industry on world markets. In fact, every adverse factor which created difficulties for Britain in the late twenties and early thirties will soon reappear in a much sharper form, as a result of the war years which brought a temporary respite.

Yet all these things so far described have been present in the long term scene for years past. I dealt with them all in my speech of resignation from the Government in May 1930, warning my fellow countrymen that a root change in the economy of Britain was becoming necessary. They have gathered momentum with the years in the normal course, but have been interrupted by two armament booms and a war, only to return with re-doubled force as the result.

All wars increase immensely the power to produce, because they release the imprisoned genius of science. And each increase in the production potential is a menace to a society which has not yet found the means to use it; means which will be discussed later in this book together with the whole question of how to evoke the full force of the scientific miracle which is now within reach of the Western mind. Over-production in relation to present market demand is soon coming back in a very big way.

But an entirely new event is now about to occur. No one should be surprised, we have all been warned. The rulers of Russia, to give them their due, in this respect have made no concealment of their intentions. The Soviets mean deliberately to break the markets of Western capitalism. The method is very simple, and they have already well practised it in a much more constructive task. Russia has accelerated the production of scientists and technicians, and consequently scientific achievements, in unprecedented degree, by depriving the rest of the population of practically every amenity of life, from decent housing to the simple mass education which prevents widespread illiteracy. The Soviet rulers have had the power to do it, and they have used that power ruthlessly, brutally. A large proportion of their total production has been removed from normal consumption and devoted to a greater speed of scientific attainment. It is a modern version of the process by which the old Pharaohs built the pyramids; a large number of people are deprived of the prime necessities of life and made to work on a project which the rulers, for purposes of ancient mysticism or modern scientific supremacy, consider to be of supreme importance.

The result is that Russia has caught up in the field of science in remarkably quick time. Now comes the next phase of the process. The toiling masses, whose compulsory sacrifice has made possible the achievement, may look forward to enjoying the fruits of their labours and self-denial. But this happy moment will again be indefinitely postponed, for the first fruits are not for them. The production of Russia's new science is not going to the home market for popular consumption; it is going to foreign markets to produce a world-wide capitalist disaster which will be even more popular with the communist masters of Russia.

Russian industry is already highly competitive in some fields, and has begun the all too simple manoeuvre. Its representatives enquire what is the lowest American or European tender in any market, and then quote 10% lower. It is quite simple if you have a population which is already well accustomed to being deprived of a large proportion of its total production for unknown purposes. And, after all, British workers put up for generations with a similar trick, more deliberately played, when finance used a large proportion of their total production in the form of capital goods to equip foreign countries, by the making of loans which created both a world financial power and a disastrous subsequent competition for British industry. The Russian workers are at least assured that when they have developed their science and destroyed world capitalism by this competition, they will in a future Soviet paradise enjoy the fruits of their labour from which so far their rulers alone have enjoyed the first taste. But whether the workers like it or not, that is what the masters are going to do. The Russians are going to allocate a large proportion of their new science's production to deliberate dumping on world markets at below the lowest possible costs of all Western nations. They have told us that they are going to do it, and they are increasingly acquiring the effective means to do it on a great scale. What is then to stop them? What answer has the West?

The answer to the Soviet system in economic and social organisation will be discussed in the next chapter, for here we are dealing only with the first necessities to meet the coming situation, which are adequate room and resources for the operation of a new system. If the countries of the West are certain to be confronted on world markets with a competition they cannot face, what is the remedy? The only possible answer is to withdraw from world markets into a viable economy, which is large enough to contain its own essential supplies and to provide its own markets. The only area available is Europe-Africa. South America is a conceivable economic alternative to Africa, but no one in the West can afford to leave a vacuum in Africa to be filled by communism, and a too close economic tie-up between Europe and South America can create political difficulties with North America which it is in the interests of the whole West to avoid. South America would appear to be rather a meeting ground for both the economies and the cultures of Europe and America.

So the creation of a Europe-African economy with considerable speed is now vital to the life of Europe. Can anyone seriously contend that time will allow fifteen years to do this; the period at present contemplated even to make the Common Market arrangements for Europe? The present way of doing things might take even longer, with Britain playing the now familiar part of a drag on the wheels. But is it possible to believe that we shall be allowed so long, in face of the circumstances cited above? Can these relatively small, isolated, individual nations of Western Europe face for fifteen years on world markets the competition of America's normal production surplus, plus the deliberate market-breaking dumping of the Soviets at below European production costs? Can they face the continually increasing Eastern competition at costs which are quite naturally below European costs, and the progressive closing of Eastern and colonial markets owing to local industrialisation? All these factors are in addition to the usual and ever sharpening internecine conflicts on world markets between European countries themselves, and the little initial problem how everyone can obtain a favourable balance of payments at the same time by selling more than they buy.

The old loan-export system by which these dilemmas were temporarily resolved at the expense of the future will find less and less sphere of operation. The areas where it might again have been developed on a great scale, such as China, are now controlled by the Soviets. And even the most innocent are unlikely for long to divest themselves of a considerable proportion of their productive wealth in order to equip Soviet industries, which will at best be used against the West for a disastrous competition and at the worst for war. The Soviets may promise not to do it, and may even offer to pay interest on loans. But who can imagine that the Soviets are going in the moment of success to betray every principle in which they have ever believed? They clearly will not do so for one moment after they have got what they want, which is rapid equipment at the expense of the West, and free equipment when loans and debts are repudiated because they need no more assistance. To expect anything else is to believe that the tiger will change overnight to a vegetarian diet, because a missionary has preached to him a sermon in favour of eating lettuces. If the animal considers vegetarianism for even a passing moment, it is only to get a better chance of eating the missionary.

Western capitalism in the modern world is likely to be deprived of the old technique of discarding a large proportion of its total production for the use of primitive countries, in return for a higher rate of loan interest than it can get at home. Such a process would not in modern reality be a loan, but a free gift; and a gift to the deadliest enemy. So the West is at last reduced to devising a system to enable its own people to consume their own production. And where can the governments of Western Europe make that system except in Europe-Africa?

This is a big task, and it must be done at speed. Can it seriously be contended that something so big can be done so quickly except by a united authority, by a European government? In final analysis, is it possible to regard all the factors of destructive competition on world markets which are now inevitable, and then to believe either that Europe will have fifteen years grace to make an alternative system or that the present governments of the individual countries will be able to make the necessary collective effort in the really short time available. If we do not believe what in the light of all experiences is an obvious absurdity, we are driven to believe that European government is a necessity. The present separate, individual governments can neither act so quickly, nor can they do anything so big. The task is nothing less than to build in Europe-Africa an economic system which is independent of world markets and supplies. That means a fundamental change in the economies of all Western countries, and a great collective effort.

It can be done; the European peoples have made an even greater effort in time of war. We must now awaken an equal enthusiasm for the tasks of peace, for the work of construction and not of destruction. To arouse that will we need a clear and a great idea, such as Europe a Nation. And to do the work we need a machine of government with the unity, efficiency, cohesion and strength which only the government of a single nation can give.

Europe, too, must regard as a single country the problems which have to be faced. If national divisions and jealousies complicate questions which are already difficult enough, they will prove insuperable. For instance, we have already briefly noted that a characteristic of the post-war period was neglect of the French position in North Africa in favour of the Suez adventure. Algeria was regarded as a purely French interest, and other Europeans not only watched the outcome with indifference but often took action to increase French difficulties. No one looked at these questions from a European standpoint. If they had regarded the Mediterranean area as Europeans, Suez would have been seen as a "life-line" which no longer led anywhere since the British Empire at the other end of it had been abandoned, and part of a line, also, which was in fact cut in the last war and which could be obliterated in a modern war. Algeria, on the other hand, was a vital point to the whole of Europe, because it could be the bridge between Europe and Africa.

Yet we chased the shadow of Suez and neglected the reality of Algeria, and the French joined the shadow-chasing because they had been baulked in defence of real European interests by an entire lack of support. Before that point, if we had faced present realities, it would have been so easy to have reached agreement with the main body of the Arabs in the Eastern Mediterranean by giving them sympathy and economic support in face of Soviet expansion, and in exchange to have obtained their assistance for a reasonable settlement in North Africa of interests which were vital to all Europe. The whole subsequent tragedy could so easily have been avoided if Europe had been united, and modern and realistic in policy. Instead Arab goodwill was thrown away by the divided nations of Europe in order to compensate British nostalgia for a lost imperial grandeur, and France for wounded feelings at her betrayal in a key position by fellow Europeans. How often in these years have we dropped the reality for the shadow.

It is the division of the European peoples, the failure to look at all problems simply from the European standpoint, which has led to all recent troubles, and is now threatening to waste the whole great European heritage in Africa. A Europe which included France could settle with the Arabs on the common sense basis that we had vital interests in some point of access to the riches of Africa, which cannot be developed without us, but that everywhere else we would support Arab interests and the economic development of their countries, in natural friendship and recognition of our mutual interest in resistance to communism.

Friendship with the Arab peoples is clearly important to the whole European position in Africa, because the Arab lands lie across European communications with that continent. And any examination of the European economic position must lead to the conclusion that we need African resources to develop a viable economy which is independent of the chaos of world markets and supplies. For that reason, in one of the very first speeches which I was able to make after the war (17 Oct 1949) I stated:

"The way to the strength, peace, prosperity of the Europeans is the development of Africa. Europe a Nation and Africa the Empire of Europe".

In this matter the whole question of colonialism and the colonial populations will have to be faced. The first need is to recognise that the old colonialism is dead. This event may be either a good or a bad thing, but for the moment that consideration is irrelevant. What matters is the fact, and the consequences have to be faced. Without the propaganda which accompanied the war and the consequent strengthening of world communism, the old colonialism might have lasted another century. It was not wise to rush backward populations along to what is called freedom so quickly, and it would certainly have been better in this respect, as in others, not to have had the war. But these things have been done, and we must live with the results.

It follows that any attempt to play the hand of the old colonialism will fail. It is an art or craft which belongs to another epoch, and whenever it has lately been attempted it has failed disastrously. A completely new attitude and policy must therefore be devised. All the present empty postures of the old colonialism must be liquidated, as soon as a new reality can be created to replace the old advantages.

The first necessity is for Europe to make up its mind collectively what is necessary to hold, and for how long. The question is, what is vital to the life of Europe, until in Europe-Africa we have had time to create a new system, which contains all its own supplies as well as its own markets? When the question is answered not in terms of individual interest but in terms of the European whole, which both transcends and comprises the lesser interests of the parts, Europe should declare plainly which of the old positions it will hold, and for how long. That collective decision and declaration will have the weight of all Europe behind it, and few will therefore be disposed to challenge it. Also a term will be set to any form of colonialism, and few will therefore wish to disturb it.

Something supported by great power for a short and definite time, is less likely to be combated than something sustained by an inadequate power for an indefinite time. In the old colonial positions which remained, all would know why we were there and for how long. They would know also that we should go directly we could, because we were building with the utmost speed a new system whose objects could be clearly explained. When it became evident that we were going in a relatively short time the pressure might not only be relaxed but reversed. When various peoples saw that we should soon no longer require their supplies, because we should have our own, they might be moved to detain rather than to speed the parting guests. The whole situation would change if Europe had a policy and acted as a unity.

All this again emphasises the necessity for European government. Without it, Europe cannot act as a unity, and we cannot regard all these matters simply from the European standpoint. All rapid and decisive development is now inhibited. For instance, it might prove to be the case that the European oil problem could be solved in the Sahara, and nowhere else so effectively; an unlikely contingency, because oil can probably be found all over the place in Africa, but it serves as an instance of cases which can be multiplied. In that event Sahara's oil supplies would be rapidly developed by the combined resources of all Europe because they were European territory. And when it came to the question of making a stand in some territory - like Algeria for instance, if it were regarded in the short or the long term as essential to European interest - it would be a very different matter if the territory in question concerned all Europe, and not one individual country which was as impoverished as the rest by present circumstances. Not only are the advantages of unity immense; they have become in present circumstances indispensable. And we cannot have the full advantages of unity without the full union which means the European government of Europe a Nation.

Further, the civilisation we intend to create must be durable and humane. This means that the blacks cannot be subjected to the whites in Africa, and exploited as a pool of cheap, inferior labour. There is plenty of room for both white and black in Africa, which is still relatively an empty continent. There is ample room for two nations, each with access to the necessary wealth for a full life and a high standard. But they must be separate nations if we are not to revert to the sweating and exploitation of the old colonialism. Whatever illusory guarantees of political liberty are given to backward peoples - even if the resistance of the white population to being in a numerical minority could be overcome, and it cannot be surmounted without the force which none are prepared to use - the less advanced peoples will in practical experience again become the bondsmen of the more advanced, if they live among them. An endless heritage of racial hatred will be the result, culminating in explosion which will be repressed with bloodshed. So it is necessary to create two nations in Africa, and no one can claim that the necessary space or wealth of potential foodstuffs and raw material are not there. Again, this is a task which is out of the question for the weak individual nations of Europe, but by no means beyond the strength and power of a united Europe.

This operation requires that a fair proportion of the total production of a united Europe should be diverted to equipping white Africa with basic capital investment, and with the machines which will enable white to replace black labour. Then adequate reward must be available for the white population which will replace the black, to attract at least one per cent of the people of Europe to migrate to Africa. No more would probably be necessary to lay the foundations of a new civilisation. This in turn would mean a revision of the whole price system for primary products now prevailing in the world, a subject which properly belongs to the next chapter. The substitution of white for black labour would turn upside down the present price structure of the African economy, and would be quite impracticable unless it were accompanied by an altogether different level of payment for primary production.

This again could only be made possible by the greater production of a united Europe, which could easily make available the necessary surplus. This mass production for a stable market could in turn only be evoked and sustained by the means described in the next chapter within a self-contained economy which rendered such measures feasible. To build a viable economy Europe must firmly decide that a proportion of the extra wealth accruing from greater production for a larger market, and from the new processes of automation, will be used to raise the reward of the primary producers. In short, we return ever to the same point: Europe cannot live without a Europe-Africa economy, and that system cannot be created except by a Europe so completely united as to have its own government. Europe a Nation is the only solution.

A further effort will be needed to create the black nation. Let no one fear that black, any more than white, will be forced to leave his home and to migrate in response to the exigencies of the new economy. That is the Soviet method, which we do not propose to follow. In the next chapter the methods of a free system are described in detail The black will be attracted in the desired direction, like the whites, by the offer of a considerably higher standard of life than he now enjoys. To achieve this he must be afforded work in the naturally rich regions which are suitable to his development, at a higher wage than he now draws. This again will be made possible by a higher payment for the primary products with which he will be mostly concerned, at any rate in the early days. Again a certain amount of capital equipment will be necessary; also a considerable number of highly-paid whites, and western-trained black technicians to assist him.

Those who are induced by large reward to take up employment for this purpose will be employed by the black nation and entirely subject to its control; there will be no trace left of the old colonialism. Whether the experiment succeeds or not remains to be seen. We should do our best to help it to succeed, and, if it did not, we should easily be able to solve our own problems in white Africa, which will be quite large and rich enough for our needs. If the black man in his own territory decides to revert to a simpler form of life, that will be his own concern, and will be no disaster either to himself or anyone else. But there is no reason to suppose that with white assistance and with the spread of education among his own people, the black man will not in due course pass through a normal development. Our duty is three-fold: to help him and not to oppress him; to give him every chance to create his own development; and to protect him from the destruction of communism.

If we are told that instead we should evacuate Africa and let it continue as a virtually empty continent of backward peoples, we reply that we are no more prepared to do this than Americans are prepared to evacuate their continent in favour of the Red Indians who, incidentally, had a better claim to priority than, for example, the Bantu in South Africa. If on the other hand we are told that black and white must grow up together in a mixed society in which the blacks are certain to be numerically superior directly they are given genuine political freedom without trickery, we reply that the system will never work, because whites who live with the problem are not prepared to work it. Also that system, in fact, under the guise of much pious humbug, would lead in practice to a very vile sweating and exploitation of the weak by the strong for the base purposes of the old capitalism. The freedom of the vote would soon be turned by skill and experience into freedom to be starved or be sweated. We do not believe in one people dominating and exploiting another; we believe in two nations living side by side in freedom and in dignity, with mutual regard and a willingness to give mutual aid.

Let those who reject the plan of Europe-Africa, inform us how the present individual countries of Europe can continue to live by open competition on the markets of the world in the face of conditions already enumerated. Let those who reject the method inform us how they can make a Europe-Africa economy in which Europeans are willing to go in adequate numbers to

Africa to make it work. They will not go if they are to become a white minority ruled by a black majority. On the other hand a black majority ruled permanently by a white minority is not something which human dignity or the conscience of modern man will indefinitely support. Therefore we are driven to the conclusion of two nations in Africa, and it is plain that only an organism so powerful as European government, with all the resources of united Europe behind it, can possibly implement it. The surplus production required to do it would be but a fraction of the production of all Europe, but it would represent an intolerable abstinence, an insupportable burden to any individual country.

From every sphere of enquiry we return to our original questions: how can something so big as Europe-Africa be made at all without European Government; how can it be done without European Government in the short time available which is certainly much less than the fifteen years now believed to be necessary to make even the common European market; and what hope is there of anything short of a united Europe with a Europe-African economy providing a solution for the economic problems now facing the nations of Western Europe? Something so big cannot be done with such speed without real unity. And real unity now means the European Government of Europe a Nation. We must now think, feel, act as Europeans.

Chapter 3

The Wage-Price Mechanism

IF a government is required to find economic solutions, it must have the means to do so. The means in modern conditions are sufficient room within which to operate. Neither a man nor a government can be held responsible for things outside their own control. Yet all the governments of present Europe are in the position of governing countries whose means of life are completely outside their control, and they make little effort to remedy their helpless situation. All these small, individual nations are dependent on external supplies of raw materials for their industries, and most of them are dependent as well on foreign foodstuffs. They are obliged to pay for these necessities by exports sold in open competition in world markets, under conditions where they have no influence whatever. Indeed, a factor as decisive as the world price level of basic commodities, or of the main manufactured goods, is in no way determined by the demand or action of the small European countries, but is almost entirely decided by the demand of America, and in the near future may also be vitally affected by the sales policy of Russia.

Whole industries in a country like Britain can at any time be put out of business by a fluctuation in world demand, or a change in the world price level, occasioned by these industrial giants whose own economies are large enough and sufficiently self-contained to be independent of world events, at least in so far as their continued economic existence is concerned. To talk of a free economy under the conditions prevailing in the present European countries is a manifest absurdity. The economies of all these nations are bound hand and foot to the economies of the larger world powers; they are thus not free but enchained to external conditions and the actions of others which they cannot control and often cannot even influence. The first necessity in developing a truly free economy is thus to become masters of our own economic destiny. For the European peoples this means the development of an economic area large enough to be viable because it contains all necessary foodstuffs and raw materials. Europe and white Africa can be such an area, and can be rapidly developed by the policy described in the last chapter.

The question now arises: what economic system should we build within that area, once we thus become free to control our own fortunes and to build an economic system suited to the European? When we have won freedom from world chaos, from the tyranny of external and uncontrollable events, let us not fall into the opposite error of creating an internal economic tyranny. It is necessary, like Russia, to have an area large enough to be independent of adverse forces in the rest of the world, but it is not necessary like the Soviets to create within that region an economic tyranny even harsher than the disruptive forces which are excluded. On the contrary, the object of our operation is to create a free economy within which men may freely enjoy the full fruits of their labour. The only question is how to make possible that full production and consumption.

Our complaint against the present system is that the beneficent force of modern scientific production is only fully used for purposes of war or preparation for war, and that full production for purposes of peace has so far only led to collapse and slump. The present system in normal conditions has never yet met and overcome the old Marxian dilemma. In plain language, the countries of the West have never yet found the means to enable their own people to consume what their own people produce.

Can this problem, then, only be overcome by the closed economy and the internal tyranny of communism? We deny this is true. We require a closed system to the extent of being independent of the world cost system, but within the necessary area it can be a free economy. What is necessary is space enough to contain our own essential supplies and to enable the economic leadership of government within that area to organise the necessary market. By free economy we mean that men should be persuaded to do what has to be done by the inducement of reward, and not compelled to do it by the means of tyranny.

I believe that economic leadership by government should be exercised through the method I have called the wage-price mechanism, which it is the purpose of this chapter to describe. This system of thinking was evolved in the empiric English fashion, when I first began seriously to consider what would happen if we had to make Europe in a hurry because the old system had collapsed. It was at once clear that if you just rolled the economies of the individual European countries together, very great problems would arise; in fact, to do it without preliminary organisation would create chaos. Wage levels in the different countries are very diverse, hours of labour and conditions of labour vary greatly, and social services diverge so completely that they impose altogether different burdens of taxation and other charges on industry. Various monopolies, restrictive practices, export subsidies and techniques of tendering by consortia, are also plentiful.

It was all these conditions, of course, which induced the statesmen of the present European governments to move so very slowly towards European Union, when they were at last reluctantly driven to the conclusion that it would eventually be necessary. We, on the other hand, felt from the outset that the complete Union of Europe was not only something ardently to be desired but a move which was urgently necessary, which must be put through in the shortest possible time before the old system collapsed for the reasons considered in the last chapter. Nothing seemed less likely than a period being allowed us so long as the fifteen years which the men of the present system require even to complete their common market. In a world where all things are possible, nothing seemed less probable than fate allowing us the grace of so much time after so many errors. Regarded from this viewpoint, therefore, the question was how to overcome by rapid and drastic action the problems which existing statesmanship hoped to circumvent by a process of slow adjustment over many years of tactful negotiation between sovereign powers and compromise agreements in cautious economic experiments.

Directly we faced the problem with any sense of urgency, it again became evident that European government was a prime necessity. To make a common market before a common government was to put the cart before the horse. On the assumption that unlimited time was available, it was, of course, possible that some form of common government would eventually grow out of common economic arrangements in the long, slow experience of learning to work together. But on the contrary premise, that present world chaos and the imminent menace of external pressure would permit no such leisurely procession towards a very vaguely defined economic objective, it again became evident that all the large and diverse problems involved could only be overcome with the decision and the speed which were necessary by the action of European government.

Thought on this problem led inevitably to larger views of the immense possibilities open to European government in command of an area so great as Europe-Africa, and animated by the guiding principle of a complete economic leadership of industry by government. Within an insulated economy independent of the world cost system, there are possibilities not merely of solving the immediate problems, but of overcoming all the long-term problems which have increasingly threatened the stability and life of present society since the beginning of the industrial revolution. We can meet all the Marxian dilemmas, and answer communism with a stronger and higher idea, which rests on freedom and inducement and not on compulsion and tyranny. This thinking emerges, therefore, not just as an answer to the immediate question of making Europe in a hurry, but as a continuous economic leadership by government in a system which overcomes modern economic and other problems without recurrence to the tyranny of the communist system.

Those who object on principle to economic leadership by government must answer the simple question, what other substantial functions governments have in modern conditions? Does a government merely exist to keep order, to keep out of war if the economic breakdown over which it has no control does not oblige war, and to transfer money from one pocket to another by taxes or the manipulation of credit? In fact, as everyone knows, government is obliged at every turn to intervene in economic matters, because economic breakdown is continually threatening the life of the country with paralysis or destruction. So government without definite principle of economic leadership is always breathlessly running behind events in an effort to catch up with the latest disaster. Is it not better, at last, clearly and frankly to face the fact that government in modern conditions must give economic leadership or cease to be a government? Should it not at least try to foresee, forestall, command and direct events, rather than always play the role of their surprised and helpless victim?

The thinking which rejects economic leadership by government is either a legacy of the days when there was no economic system because life was primitive enough to conduct itself, or is a revulsion from the economic system of communism, and its less effective camp follower, democratic and bureaucratic socialism, because that system conditions the mind and soul of man under guise of regulating his economic fortunes. The modern view, on the other hand, is that government is obliged by present circumstances to lead men in the organisation of their economic life as the only means of preserving for them freedom from poverty and a chance to enjoy their private lives. In principle it must be obvious that in modern conditions government cannot wash its hands of economic matters. And directly we realise this it becomes clear that it is better for government in economic affairs to lead rather than to follow, to be the first master of events rather than the first victim.

So we begin with the premise of a definite, conscious and deliberate economic leadership by government. Let us see how it works out in practice under present conditions, initially in the making of Europe and finally in a system of a continuous and persistent guidance of civilisation to ever higher levels.

To make Europe rapidly the first necessity is for economic leadership by government to create comparable conditions in similar industries throughout the Continent. Otherwise we shall be held up for ever by fear of unfair competition. Nations cling to protective devices and to delays which in practice will be protracted long beyond even the statutory fifteen years. We shall never make Europe until we take the plunge into the water, and that plunge is the making of European government. The first task of that government will be to render delay and protection unnecessary by raising wages in low-paid areas, shortening hours where they are unduly long, and securing some uniformity of social systems and consequent charges on industry. It is necessary to secure comparable conditions in comparable industries throughout, in order to prevent the undercutting and collapse of industries in areas enjoying a relatively higher standard of life. This is the first and minimum requirement, and even it will not finally be secured without the conscious and deliberate action of government.

There is more to it, of course, than simply the publishing of edicts to raise wages and shorten hours in certain regions. There is much more to it than just taking the plunge in the sense of letting the free play of economic forces do the rest. For instance it is sometimes argued that if we could just persuade all the European peoples to roll their economies together, nature and the free play of economic forces would do all that was necessary. It is contended that labour would flow naturally from low to high-paid areas, and that employers in the low-paid areas would be compelled to raise wages and to improve conditions in order to retain any labour at all.

But it is not difficult to conceive the friction which this would inevitably create, and the ensuing chaos. Even the suggestion of a few Italian and Hungarian miners being introduced into British mines was enough to produce a ferment. Time, and experience of a new system, will be needed to remove the old fears of a pool of cheap labour threatening to undercut the whole level of a higher standard of life. And if in fact these things are just left to chance and the free play of economic forces, something of the kind might well result. The unscrupulous employer might welcome a reserve of migratory labour on which he could draw for the purpose of cheapening costs in his own high-cost labour area. On the other hand, an employer in the low-paid areas, with the best will in the world, would not be able to raise wages to retain his labour force without a capital equipment comparable to that prevailing in the high paid area.

The result of simply making a complete common market coupled with the entire freedom and mobility of labour might well be to denude the poorer areas of labour and to reduce the standard of life in the richer areas. It would become a Trade Unionist's nightmare, and European Trade Unionism - whose co-operation we seek at every turn in this matter - is quite right to insist on a real and complete planning of the business. In fact, common market, mobility of labour and investment policy must go together, and that means plan, action and leadership by government. Capital equipment must be available to the lower-paid areas in order to make their industries still competitive when they pay higher wages. The guarantee that the same high wages will be paid to comparable industries throughout the whole region must be available to industries in the high-standard areas when they expose themselves to the free competition of common market.

There will be no problem created by the rush of cheap labour from one area to another if wages are the same in similar industries throughout all Europe, because few men will leave their home country if they can there enjoy as high a standard of life as elsewhere. But to enable such wages to be paid in the poorer areas capital equipment must be supplied to put them on an equal footing with their richer competitors; we want no battle within Europe between sweated labour without equipment and highly-paid labour with proper machinery. Still less do we want an economic fight between high and low-paid labour with the same machinery, because that would attract unscrupulous capital to the lower-paid areas of Europe as the same conditions have already done to the lower-paid areas of the East. Wages must be determined throughout by government, and that action must be linked to a planned investment and development policy. The common market will encounter all these problems directly it becomes seriously organised, and in the end they can only conceivably be overcome by a common government.

The purpose of government must ever be to lead and not to control. It is not necessary in such an economy for government to do more than to determine wages, and also to fix prices in conditions where monopoly prevails to the extent of eliminating the ordinary corrective of competition. These two principles are essential; they are the basis of the wage-price mechanism. They are the means by which government can lead the whole economy at first in the clearly necessary direction and later in the desirable direction. With these two simple powers - simple in principle - everything can be done, and without them nothing can be done. Yet they are powers denied to government by all parties and by all economic thinking.

The additional measures which are necessary to support this action such as government-assisted investment, are already a recognised principle; the only difference in these proposals in this respect is that assistance would be given in Europe which today is reserved almost exclusively for the Far East and for the more primitive peoples of Africa. In principle there is nothing new in this suggestion.

But the policy of the wage-price mechanism is a revolutionary departure from previous principle and practice. Nothing of the sort has been done before, or even suggested in political programmes. In Great Britain wage boards have prevented the extremes of sweating in certain depressed industries, while in America and elsewhere a minimum wage law has prevented wages falling below a certain level in the lower-paid categories of industry. There have also been some attempts to peg wages above the economic level within systems not large or developed enough to be viable, and to back the process with the fatal device of inflation.

But government has never intervened to determine wages in every category of industry as a conscious and deliberate means of shaping the whole economy in the fashion desired, within a system large enough to contain its own foodstuffs, raw materials and potential market. What is new in this policy is the idea that government should exercise continuous economic leadership by the determining of wages in every sphere of industry and when necessary by the fixing of prices.

In a fully functioning Europe-Africa economy it should not often be necessary to fix prices except in monopoly conditions; a large economy makes possible freedom. But in anything approaching a siege economy, which long persistence in present policies may bring to Britain, it may also be necessary to fix prices over a wide field. The wage-price mechanism is a flexible instrument which can be adapted rapidly to the diverse conditions of crisis and prosperity. In the great economy of Europe the means would be used only to lead a free and expanding economy; finally it will be found that both freedom and prosperity are out of the question in any lesser area.

So far we have seen in brief how it would work in overcoming the immediate problems arising from a rapid making of Europe. It would be indispensable for the elimination of unfair competition within Europe which would bring chaos, if wages were not made uniform in comparable industries by action of government. Let us now see how the same principles would apply to older and deeper problems.

The equation of production and consumption has been the major problem of the industrial age, particularly in later developments. In fact, the question has only been solved at all by wars, armament booms, foreign loans which in many cases have simply been charity in recent times, but were previously weapons in the battle for foreign markets, and by government expenditure on every conceivable purpose good and bad, which had the ultimately simple object of discarding the production of which modern society is capable. These were all the desperate and dangerous expedients by which a bankrupt system sought to escape from the basically simple problem which had always baffled it, how to enable its own people to consume what its own people produced.

This is the thing which government has never been able to do in normal times and in a normal way. Economic leadership through the wage-price mechanism can enable government to do this for the first time, in a regular, systematic and scientific method. If government has an area of operation large enough to be independent of the world cost system and is equipped with such powers, it is possible to equate production and consumption. The power of the people to consume goods can be increased equally and simultaneously with the power of science to produce goods. Wages, salaries and all forms of reward for creative work of any kind can be increased as the potential supply of goods increases in order to give a market commensurate with the production. The prime problem of modern industrial society can be solved with relative ease.

Modern science makes nonsense of the old argument at the beginning of the industrial revolution that goods could only be produced economically in the area most naturally suited to their production, and then could only be economically exchanged with other goods similarly produced in corresponding areas. Now it is possible to produce almost any goods anywhere at equal cost, granted some equality in labour cost and market. Size of market is now a far greater factor in cost than natural conditions. It does not much matter any longer whether you have a humid atmosphere or any other natural conditions which happen to be required for a particular kind of production, because that can be artificially created, but it does matter immensely whether you have a market large enough to justify and therefore to evoke mass production. In most modern industries the rate of production for a mass market is much more important even than the rate of wage.

What matters therefore above all else is the great market, and that depends on two factors: the size of the area and the purchasing power of the population. Again we secure both these necessary conditions by the creation of Europe-Africa and by the economic leadership of government through the wage-price mechanism. Government then becomes completely free to meet and to overcome the chief menace of modern industrial society; the chronic tendency in normal conditions to over-produce in relation to the available market with the consequence of recurrent economic crises and a continual threat of mass unemployment.

Too simple, will reply the sophisticated critic, as always when confronted with one of the root truths; he is invariably the prisoner of the complications which always grip minds that have not yet been able to penetrate to the essentials. Most things begin in a complicated way, before men really begin to understand the problems. Scientific and industrial developments provide many examples of this, which can also be found in the region of pure thought. And still more in economic matters, it is an error to believe that because men are held tight in the grip of involved complexities, the final solution cannot present a relatively simple principle.

A completely new way of economic thinking will in any case soon be compelled by the development of automation. The problem has long been germinating; it was one of the main themes of my speech of resignation from the government in 1930. In those days, however, it was known as rationalisation, and the increasing displacement of men's labour by machinery was already threatening the whole existing structure of industrial society. At that time the constant tendency existed for supply to outstrip demand, and it was clear that the new process would accentuate the problem. More goods would be produced with the labour of less men, and a market which was already inadequate might be further diminished by mass unemployment with a consequent further loss of purchasing power. Again the question has been masked for years by wars and armament booms, but the problem returns with normal conditions in an aggravated form.

Now it is not merely a question of machinery displacing some men, but of machinery replacing altogether the labour of men. We are approaching the age in which most labour will be performed by machines serviced by relatively small bands of highly trained specialists. Under the old economics these few specialists would draw enormous wages, and the rest would be unemployed. No market would then exist for the ever-increasing products of the machines which would pile up in the midst of a surrounding waste of poverty. Such is the logical reduction to absurdity of a system which has never devised any effective means of distributing the wealth which modern science can produce.

We begin again to meet the automation problem with our two premises of the viable area and the economic leadership of government through the wage-price mechanism. And again by this means we can raise wages, salaries and all forms of reward for all kinds of work and service to the point that the market is able to absorb by effective demand even the product of an almost complete automation. It is, of course, obvious that it is inadequate simply to raise the wages of those engaged in automatic industry, though under present conditions this is about all that would happen. To provide a market for the greatly increased production it will be necessary greatly to increase wages in all the primary industries and basic services.

For instance, not only is it fair considerably to increase agricultural wages and profits, miners' wages, and all wages in comparable industries, but it would be absolutely necessary in these conditions if modern industries were not to collapse for lack of a market.

The Wage-Price Mechanism

The defence forces, civil servants and others employed in basic services, whose conditions would not be so much affected by automation, must all have their reward greatly raised if market demand is to increase in proportion to the increase in production occasioned by that process. Under conditions of full automation the old question of how little you can pay such people will yield to the new question of how much you must pay them to keep things going at all. It is time our thinking became prepared for some of the new paradoxes of the coming age of science.

It is, of course, true today that if you raise the wages of those employed in the primary industries and basic services, you increase the cost of living and consequently increase industrial costs. The result is inability to compete successfully in the dog-fight of foreign markets against countries with a lower standard of life. Wages are held down by the necessities of international competition far below the level which is necessary to provide a market for the modern industries of automation. So the end is always lack of market demand, and slump. But in a system governed by our two premises, we shall be entirely free from the world cost system and all under-cutting of low wage competition on world markets, and free consequently for action by government to raise the standard of life within our own system until consumption equates production at any level which scientific development has reached.

A far bigger total pool of wealth will be available for distribution when mass production industries with a full automation technique have been organised for such a market; as they inevitably will be directly such a market exists and greater reward can thereby be won. It will then not only be desirable but necessary that primary producers like agriculture and the basic services shall participate very fully in the distribution of that larger amount of wealth. In these conditions it will not be a question of the town worker doing without, or paying more than he can afford in order to give the farmer and farm worker a fair price, but only a question of the farming community having a fair share in a larger total.

This will, of course, entail a rise in the cost of primary products and these basic services to the rest of the community, but in these conditions this will not be an inflation but an adjustment of reward between different sections of the community; it will not jeopardise our economy. We have noted the first reason for this immunity is that we shall be free from the world cost system, and the rise in our costs in certain respects will, therefore, not endanger our competitive position. We shall no longer need to be competitive abroad, because a balance of payments problem will no longer exist. The second reason is that those engaged in productive industry will be producing far more than before, and will consequently be able to enjoy far higher rewards; they will therefore be able to afford a rise in certain costs.

A rise of costs in some cases will, of course, be offset by a fall of costs in other cases, where a higher rate of production for a larger market operates. But in principle we must always be ready to face a rise in particular costs, and we shall have the means to do it. When automation, and further development of the present mass-production technique have greatly expanded production for a completely assured market, the wage-price mechanism will, in effect, enable government to syphon off the surplus from a larger pool of distributable wealth in any direction desired.

In addition to the cases already mentioned some proportion of the new wealth should clearly go to the large and important category of those performing diverse individual services - ranging from big accountants to small shop-keepers, and covering a multiplicity of other occupations - who would certainly be entitled to charge more. In fact, it would be desirable that they should do so, in order to spread evenly the new purchasing power. The new wealth must not coagulate in lumps, but be more evenly distributed.

The same pool of new resources could be made available to prevent hardship to pensioners and others living on small fixed incomes, who might be affected by a rise of cost in some commodities, although, as we have seen, they would be assisted by a fall in the price of other goods. We will examine shortly the question whether any remaining doubt exists that under such a system a larger total volume of wealth would be available for such purposes.

To return first to the vital question of agriculture, both a wage and a price mechanism will be wanted in this sphere. Wages will have to be raised, both to attract and to retain labour on the land in these conditions and to provide a demand for the greatly increased output of automation and mass-producing industry for an assured market. But in this case, prices will also have to be fixed by government, partly on account of monopoly conditions - agriculture if so organised could clearly become a monopoly capable of holding the whole community up to ransom, the only surprising thing is that farmers have not yet acted together more strenuously to defend themselves - and also because it will be necessary for government, by the fixing of prices, to evoke the particular forms of agricultural production which are necessary in rapidly changing conditions.

The experience of the British Marketing Board system can here be very valuable. There is no reason why this system should not be developed to cover all Europe. Agriculture throughout the Continent could thus be given the stability and assured market which is necessary to the industry, and the present reluctance of agriculturists to join the European community would quickly be changed to enthusiasm for a development they would recognise as advantageous. Prices would need to be declared well in advance, because in such a long-term business planning must be well ahead.

The farmer is sensitive to variations in the price-level in spite of the long-term nature of his business, and experience shows that production can be effectively directed by this means. It will be necessary for government through this mechanism to give economic leadership in agriculture during the rapidly developing conditions of the new Europe, because that development will bring great changes in existing demand. As industrial workers become better off, their desires for foodstuffs will change; for instance less bread and more meat will probably be eaten. Such developments must be anticipated by government, and directed by variations in the price level of diverse products to secure the necessary variation in the kind of foodstuffs grown. There is no sphere in which the wage-price mechanism is more necessary than agriculture, and no region in which it can bring greater benefits to the producer.

The fear of agriculture to enter Europe today is the fear of a sensible man to enter chaos. But in the system we are here describing agriculture's basic necessity of stability and long-term planning can be the premise of all action. In terms of the general economy the most important thing of all is to use some part of the extra wealth derived from the new method to bring the primary producers to a higher standard of life. There is not the slightest doubt that all primary producers in such an economy must have their reward raised, not only absolutely but relatively. Otherwise we shall not attract men to the land and the primary industries, and we shall not secure the broad and stable market for all production which is necessary.

It will also be essential to open out virgin Africa, and to pay men large rewards to do this arduous work. Those who go out as pioneers will be paid not less but more than others. In this respect again the whole premises of our economic thinking must be revised. Otherwise we shall not get the men for the job of opening up the new areas which are vital to a system that must be independent of the economic dislocation incurred by selling and buying on external markets. We must have a balance between pioneer, primary industries and the main body of the coming automation industries, and to secure this we have to pay these primary producers a reward out of all relation to their present remuneration. We must lead and draw men back to the land and the great primary occupations in the new continent of Africa with the inducement of higher reward.

The Wage-Price Mechanism

By means of the wage-price mechanism government can promote any major economic development, through deliberately raising wages in a certain area of industry relative to other industries, and thus can attract labour in the desired direction. This is a very vital factor in the leadership and guidance of the entire economic system, which operates in addition to the other great advantage of releasing the full power of modern scientific production which is today inhibited. The wage-price mechanism can guide the economy, organise a market and in so doing evoke full production, and from the greater resources thus created can give a true equilibrium to the economy by paying better those employed in the primary industries, basic services and other vital categories of industry and national life which we have considered.

But some may still doubt whether a larger pool of distributable wealth will be available in these conditions, from which government can draw the means so to shape and direct the new economy. Those who deny this is possible must show that it is impossible for modern science greatly to increase the production of wealth for an assured market which increases pari passu with production. Any man who attempts that demonstration begins by confessing his ignorance of the present facts, as well as the potential of modern industry. Let anyone who denies the connection between mass-production for a great and assured market and a greater share of wealth per head, explain the disparity between earnings and the standard of life in America and the poor and divided European countries today.

Our science, technique and skill are at least equal to their capacity; all that we lack is the market which they enjoy. And under these proposals we would not merely possess a large area like America of unorganised and fitful demand, but would be producing for the progressive but stable demand of a market organised to march in step with the advance of science. Anything achieved in America could be easily out-stripped by the energy of the Europeans released to operate in these conditions. Two things are certain: the first that we can enormously increase production for such a market

63

and consequently the total of distributable wealth, the second that we cannot just leave the whole of this great achievement to the forces of chaos. All means are there, but they must be organised. The economic leadership of government is essential.

These great forces of modern science create possibilities of a standard of life far beyond anything hitherto conceived, if they have adequate direction and room for their operation. They are potentially beneficial to an extraordinary degree, but they can be almost as dangerous in the economic as in the military sphere. Life has become too big to be left to chance. Government cannot abdicate in face of the modern economic problems. These are forces which cannot be left to the freaks of chaos.

In the past, the long slow operation of economic forces in the end provided the adjustment necessary in society, albeit with much waste and unnecessary suffering. But things are now moving too fast; science brings constant changes at a speed which requires not subsequent adjustment but anticipation and preliminary organisation. In such a situation government must act, and in broad principle government has two methods of action: leadership or compulsion, persuasion or tyranny.

Communism has solved the problem in a fashion by the latter method. When science brings a revolutionary change, there is no time lost in persuading men to adapt themselves to it, or in waiting until the pressure of economic circumstances brings a natural adaptation as in the past. If a new scientific development, or a strategic requirement, demand the development of a new industrial area in Siberia, whole villages of workers in western Russia are told to collect what things they can carry, mount a train and go to their new task. Under these conditions it is easy to keep pace in a certain way with the march of science.

But these are not methods which would be tolerated in the West, or that any sane man would seek to employ. Are we simply, then, to wait until the blows of economic fact compel us to adjust ourselves to new development of science? Must we always defer action until old industries are abruptly ruined and men thrown into unemployment? Must government always trot laggardly behind scientific development and economic fact, merely trying to mitigate the resultant hardship with a little organised charity which is given the resounding name of a new form of society? Is there no choice except tyranny or laisser-faire, nothing between the position of the bully and the victim?

Cannot government become master of economic circumstance and place itself in command of the great force of modern science, by means of leadership and not compulsion? Again we reply that the wage-price mechanism is the means to this end. Once we have established a viable area which is free from external economic interference, government can lead, direct and mould the whole economy as it wishes, with this instrument and under these conditions. In the same way by determining wages and insisting that the community - within an insulated system - pays more for certain specialised services from the larger resources available, the government can effectively lead the whole economy in other desirable directions.

Through the wage-price mechanism, also, the essential differential in reward for skill and responsibility can be restored and even accentuated. Once the power of determining wages is granted, government can insist that throughout the whole body of industry men with special skill and undertaking particular responsibilities shall receive a far higher level of reward. The present tendency to drag all down to a common level, in which skill and the acceptance of responsibility count for practically nothing, is bound finally to result in the end of any human society because it denies every law of the nature to which we are all subject. Civilisation, in mitigating the brutality of nature, must not eliminate its incentives.

If we do not pay more to skill, or to those who carry responsibility, men will not acquire the one nor accept the other. Government must fearlessly explain to the people the necessity to pay highly for special skill and particular character; it is a point which the mass of the people very clearly understands and appreciates. Few and diseased are the types who desire to tear down and to destroy anyone who can do something they cannot do, or who possesses things they do not possess, and they gravitate naturally to the form of politics where they can give expression to this malady. But the great generous mass of the people are still free from the cancer of decadence which is jealousy, and are very ready to admire and reward the man who can do a good job.

Government with the power of economic leadership and the ability to explain what it is doing, would find no difficulty in restoring through the wage-price mechanism a system of differential reward far higher than has ever hitherto existed. For this is a prime necessity if we are to get the best from men of ability. Above all in the decisive, world-shaping sphere of science it is necessary to match ability with reward. This is a subject at which I have hammered ever since I was a young minister in the Government of 1929, and before that in the effort to secure a realist programme for the socialist movement in Britain. In 1947 I wrote that statesmen in this age should live and work with scientists as the Medicis lived and worked with artists. If that view had been accepted, the governments of the West would surely not have found themselves today in the pitiful position of a man possessing every natural advantage and yet outstripped in the race of life by others who possess nothing but the determination which he lacks.

So within a system of differential reward, which the great power of the wage-price mechanism will make possible to a degree never before contemplated, the reward of the scientist must be lifted to a level commensurate with his function, which is the first in the state under government. Honour, too, must go to men who, like soldiers, are moved as much or more by honour as by reward. And science must also be consciously and deliberately brought into the councils of government. We envisage a future in which men called to rule will be part statesman, part scientist. Until then we must find statesmen who know enough of science to work with scientists, and scientists who know enough of politics to work with statesmen. The two subjects are interlocked in fact, and must become interlocked by deliberate organisation in the theory and practice of the State. All these great possibilities will be assisted by a power which enables men to be rewarded according to the creative work they do.

Before we consider further possibilities of the method under discussion, it might now be convenient to summarise what has so far been suggested. The purposes of economic leadership through the wage-price mechanism which we have so far envisaged are in brief the following:

(1) The equation of wages in comparable industries which is necessary in the rapid construction of Europe, if we are to avoid under-cutting and unfair competition in the internal market.

(2) The general raising of wages in equal proportion and with uniformity in comparable industries as science makes possible an increase in general productive capacity which will consequently require a larger market.

(3) The payment of a higher reward both absolutely and relatively to those engaged in the primary industries such as agriculture and pioneer developments in Africa, also to all employed in basic services like the defence forces, the civil services, etc., with the dual object of attracting men of the best calibre to these essential purposes, and also of increasing and enlarging the market which will be required by automation and by industries which are organised for mass production in the assured and stable conditions of the new system.

(4) The securing of differential rewards in high degree for skill and responsibility throughout industry, and particularly in spheres like science, where it is vital to encourage the development of the

higher talents. For all these purposes the use of the wage-price mechanism is not only legitimate but essential.

The question of profit now arises; if you will determine wages will you also determine profit? The first answer is that the wage-price mechanism automatically determines profit, to the extent that this is necessary for the health of the economy. Profit is, in considerable degree, determined directly you determine wages; and the additional power to determine prices when necessary, can make certain that the profit principle is kept within the bounds of the desirable incentive and is prevented from becoming profiteering.

We will shortly examine how a government which studies the interests of the workers and of the whole community, can easily prevent by the wage-price mechanism the undue accumulation of profit at the expense of general purchasing power which can finally upset an economic system. Such economic leadership can provide a direct and simple answer to one of the main Marxian dilemmas.

It would also, of course, be possible to fix differential profits for different categories of industry in the same way as we fix differential wages. But at this point we should tend to cramp initiative, and to check the beneficent forces of natural intelligence and energy, if we did not allow a man to make any profit he could provided he paid the fair wages laid down for his industry. Our system rests on encouraging and therefore rewarding the creative capacities of men. Let a man make profit for himself, provided he pays his workers properly and by his creative work serves the community as well as himself. Through the wage-price mechanism we can always ensure that he pays his workers properly. In fact, we can determine by this means that a very fair share in the profits goes to the workers. But the detailed control of profits can entail a reversion to the bureaucracy we wish above all to avoid, and would tend inevitably to destroy the invention, initiative and energy which are precisely the forces we need to make the driving force of the new and expanding system.

The Wage-Price Mechanism

Conditions may well arise in the divided and helpless states of the present Europe, in which all purchasing power will have to be frozen - wages, profits, rent, interest and everything else - while the whole economy is put on a siege basis for the purposes of survival. And no government faced with the condition of collapse should hesitate for a moment to take this firm and decisive action when necessary. I have elsewhere described the measures necessary if this painful situation should arise through delay in entering the European economy.

But in the new Europe of vast resources and unlimited potential such action would be not only unnecessary and intolerable, but entirely self-defeating. We are faced now with the problem of poverty economics in small separate countries living under the necessity to sell enough in the dog-fight of world markets to buy the essential foodstuffs and raw materials they cannot produce at home. We shall be faced on the other hand with the contrary problem of plenty economics, when 300 million people have come together to organise the unlimited resources of the two great continents of Europe and Africa for their mutual benefit. We shall then pass from the period of restriction to the period of expansion. In those conditions we shall not want to stop men making money, but to encourage them to make money provided they are working, producing and creating for the benefit of the whole community as well as themselves.

The business of government through the economic leadership of the wage-price mechanism will be then to organise an adequate market and to see that the workers get a fair share, not to interfere with the creative individual or to rob him of his fair profits. In short, wages must be determined because the workers cannot look after themselves, except in the transient and rare condition of an inflationary market for their labour which is in itself a symptom of coming collapse. Despite all the great work of Trade Unionism in the last half century, they have usually been far from getting their fair share, or even share enough to maintain the economic equilibrium of the State. The makers of profit, on

69

the other hand, need no looking after if they get anything like the fair conditions we propose to establish; if they are any good at the job they can look after themselves well enough.

The danger in the past of a chaotic capitalism has been such great accumulations of profit that the whole economy became unbalanced; more profit was often made than individuals were even capable of spending on themselves, despite extremes of luxury spending which were not only a disgrace in comparison with the surrounding poverty, but which twisted and deformed the whole body of the economy. The surplus above what they were capable of spending was often used for speculation of an anti-social kind, or left in cash and not invested at all. Yet undoubtedly in the past the whole progress of the system depended on this principle of a great accumulation of profit, much of which was used for productive investment. In addition to its other vices the system could not function without the continual waste of speculation and luxury spending which accompanied this useful process.

All these things are capable not only of correction but of being kept continually in proper balance by the wage-price mechanism, and will under our system be subject to the general guidance of government. Undue accumulations of wealth can be naturally and automatically checked, by the simple process of raising wages to take a larger share of the profits of industry, if any such tendency should develop to a dangerous or undesirable extent.

Again, through the self-governing bodies of industry which we will shortly consider, it will be possible to implement the general policy of government by establishing definite proportions in the various industries between wages, profit and investment. All three factors would benefit in equal proportion when the introduction of greater efficiency or a general expansion of the market brought greater reward to the industry as a whole. In many cases it would not be necessary, once things got going, that investment should increase proportionately with the other two factors; and the chief benefit of improvement and expansion would therefore accrue to wages and profits whose interest in this prosperity would be mutual.

Another great sphere where the leadership but not the control of government can be exercised is in the region of credit and the general operation of banking. At present, banking is a bugbear to progressive thinkers. The reason is that this power has on occasion been the master and not the servant of the community. Within the international system it exercises a decisive power, because the flight of capital in one way or another despite all nominal restrictions is possible so long as international trading on world markets continues, and this ability gives to finance the power to break governments and consequently to control them. But again, within a closed system - closed, albeit the area is so great that in a few years with the aid of science its production may outstrip that of the whole world today - the rule of finance will cease, because it cannot fly away and in the process destroy the economic system which it deserts.

On the other hand a greater freedom will exist for the individual than he possesses today. There will be no valid reason why a man in Europe-Africa should not exchange his fortune in those lands for the fortune of another man in America. The economic effect would be nil; strange as the thought may seem to someone accustomed to the strict controls which the international system now makes necessary. If it is no longer necessary to buy or sell goods on the markets of the world - because all necessary goods and all markets are self-contained - it will not be possible for finance by a flight of capital to break the exchange, for the good reason that the exchange on any appreciable scale will not exist. These are novel thoughts, and we cannot here pause to examine them at length, but they will be found under the closest analysis in these conditions to be valid.

Creative finance and banking, on the other hand, will be able to derive greater reward than ever in the constructive task of developing the backward areas of Europe and opening up the virgin territories of Africa. Never were the imagination and ability of creative bankers more needed; if they do the job, they will deserve and will earn rewards which will make trivial the present scratchings of small speculations on the exchanges of a failing international system. There is more to be made by able and honest banking in the construction of two continents than in the demolition of an old and decomposing system.

Other new possibilities are open within a self-contained system of large area and unlimited potential resources. It might be advisable to develop a system of differential credit. Basic services like housing might be charged a lower rate of interest on a loan which could be amortised over a short period of years; the result would be to slash the cost of house building and of rents, as everyone is aware who has studied the costing of house building. On the other hand purposes which are less socially desirable could be charged a much higher rate of interest, which would balance the low rate charged to necessities.

But again the whole bias of this writer is in favour of freedom and against the interference and control which would lead us back to bureaucracy. Let us by all means charge a low rate of interest for basic services like housing, but not seek too much to direct and to control those who want credit for making other things. It may be necessary to charge these people more for their credit, but it should not be necessary to tell them what to do with it. Some bad things will be done, but also many good things. And it is better in a strong, rich and expanding system of unlimited opportunity to have mistakes made, and even to have a few anti-social things done, than to have an old hag of a universal governess sitting on everybody's shoulder and telling him what he may do and what he may not do. Let us set people free to do and to create; let the great force of nature work.

This sphere of banking for a new system should, of course, be a subject for consideration by many expert minds in banking, industry and government. At this early stage it seems possible that within such a closed system, with a definite economic leadership, we might develop both a normal banking and a venture banking. The former would operate at a low level of interest for people whose reward would be naturally more limited, while the latter would operate on a higher level of interest for risk purposes which would naturally command a far greater profit, in fact an unlimited reward if successful. We might in relatively short-term credit operations develop as well the outlook of the prudent long-term investor, who reasonably expects a higher return on his money for a risky than for a safe enterprise. Banking in a richer and more enterprising system might break away from a frozen dependence on collateral security, and become a participant in industry's great adventure.

Above all we must find the means either through public or private finance to back the inventor, and carry new enterprises through from the crude experiment to the market stage. Again all these things will be far easier within an insulated system, under a definite economic leadership in which all resources and all credit based upon them will be available for the development of Europe-Africa and for no other purpose.

General credit policy must, of course, keep the price level stable. Much greater production for an assured market would cause a fall in the price level, without credit expansion. Deflation is almost as undesirable as inflation, and the aim of credit policy would be again to prevent this by keeping the price level stable.

The prices of individual commodities might rise for reasons already examined, but this rise would be more than offset by a fall in the price of other commodities produced by industries with a greater turn-over for a larger but, internally, still competitive market. Again, the self-contained character of the economy would make it relatively easy for credit policy to keep the general price level stable and to avoid inflation.

Nothing so rots the whole economy or the individual character as inflation. This condition is the curse alike of the industrialist and the worker seeking to do an honest job; the former in this situation depends for his reward more on his capacity as a speculator than a producer, and the latter suffers the misery of his wages always chasing prices. The speculator is king of the great world, and the spiv is the prince of the underworld. Every value thus fashioned is the opposite of the values we desire.

Within a large and insulated economy such as we recommend, it is, of course, relatively easy for a responsible credit policy to keep the price level stable. The inflation of today derives mainly from the balance of payments problem under which all the small, divided countries of Europe suffer at present, on account of the lack of any adequate supply of foodstuffs and raw materials within their borders. The whole life of such countries depends on their export trade, because without sufficient exports they cannot buy the imports of food and raw materials which are essential to their existence.

So the export trade must be kept going at any cost, even at the cost of a cost inflation which is today much more common than the old-fashioned demand inflation, whereby the general supply of money exceeded the general supply of goods. Today wages are pushed up out of all proportion in particular trades on which the life of the export system depends, because government dares not risk trouble in these industries and will always pay up rather than fight. The process of paying up, in the nationalised industries in particular, is financed by some directly inflationary devices. Modern inflation, in short, is usually a surrender to blackmail, by a government which dares not risk any disturbance of the export trade because it is faced with an acute balance of payments problem. Such problems will not exist under our system, again for the simple reason that an external balance of payments will not exist.

Consequently a firm and balanced credit policy can be consistently pursued. Government will even be in a strong enough position deliberately to stimulate demand by credit policy when this is desirable. All the present fears of a semi-siege economy will be a thing of the past. On occasion it will be right to raise wages and to supply credit for this purpose, in anticipation of greater production and not merely as an accompaniment. There is no reason why credit should not temporarily finance new demand in the same way that it today finances new enterprise. The credit will cease when greater production matches the greater demand, just as now the credit normally ceases when a new enterprise becomes productive and profit earning. None of these things can be done today within the little European countries living in daily dread of any temporary increase of costs upsetting their competitive positions on world markets. But within a large and insulated economy, entirely independent of world supplies and markets, we can also give credit leadership in a constructive policy.

We could even endure that supreme luxury of freedom or of licence, strikes. No sensible government would ever withhold any liberty which does not threaten the life of a nation. And the right to withdraw labour has long been regarded as one of the basic liberties. Under the system we propose a strike could be a nuisance but would not be a fatality. A protracted or even an extensive strike in some area of Europe a Nation would not destroy nor even greatly affect the life of 300 million people, provided government performed the first duty of all governments in keeping the essential services going. At present a strike in key industries can be a death stroke to a small nation struggling with a delicate balance of payments problem. It could in the system we propose be only a nuisance, and liberty is worth many a nuisance.

In practice, strikes on any large scale would soon cease to exist, because responsible trade union leaders would be far more interested in developing a system of much benefit to their members than in using the once necessary but soon obsolete weapons of a previous epoch. Yet another opportunity will then occur to translate a phrase into a reality. Trade Unions are sometimes described in England today as another "estate of the realm". Under our system they would have the chance in truth and in fact to become it.

This is not the place to describe, except in general terms, an administrative machine; I have done this before in some detail. But it is plain that in the system we desire - a system free from bureaucratic control - the Trade Unions must be invited to play a vital part together with the employers' organisations in the detailed administration of the wage-price mechanism, under the general economic leadership of government. The representatives of government, employers and trade unions should work together in a constantly functioning administrative machine to implement that economic leadership of government; they would naturally be assisted much by bodies like the Department of Scientific and Industrial Research in England and the various trade research organisations of all European countries. The trade unions' and employers' organisations which already exist, could be a basis of the necessary administrative machine.

Wherever possible it is wise to use existing machinery and to develop it to new and larger purposes. We must above all avoid bureaucracy, detailed control and, as far as possible, compulsion in general administration. The only element of compulsion will be the determining of wages and some prices by government; that is the new and revolutionary principle from which all else follows. Organisations composed of employers, trade unionists and government representatives will be required to carry out the law in this respect. In all other matters government should rely on the voluntary co-operation of employers and trade unions, and should do its utmost by constant consultation to evoke it.

It is not so difficult to secure voluntary co-operation in a constantly expanding system of vast extent and possibility, when the question is not how to cut down the standard of life in order to live at all in competition on world markets, but how to open up immense new resources without menace of external interference, and how to organise a market for the enjoyment of a greatly increased means of production. In these conditions either an employer or trade union leader who refused to co-operate by reason of political prejudice would very speedily find himself displaced by the votes of his fellows, who would be more interested in securing a better life in the future than in venting the spites of the past. Let us take all good men and all good ideas - in whole or in part - from both present and past.

Let us not be deterred by prejudice or misrepresentation from examining, for example, some of the methods of the corporate system, which could be employed in its co-operative but not in its compulsory aspects in the larger and more favourable conditions of our system. English liberalism approached much the same position under the name of co-partnership; terminology and prejudice count for far too much in these matters.

The more advanced method of syndicalist organisation, which we now propose only for industries at present nationalised, can be more conveniently studied in a later chapter. But if it be adopted, the same principle of administrative machinery could operate so far as the wage-price mechanism was concerned. Any number of different administrative systems could in fact be devised to implement the basic principle of economic leadership by government through the wage-price mechanism. There is no disputing that the administrative side is feasible; the only question is the choice of method. We shall choose always the method which involves the minimum bureaucratic interference with industry. We interfere at only one point, but it is the decisive point of determining wages, and sometimes prices.

Is not this the very minimum action the coming period requires? We are entering the age of unlimited power from the new development of science and of a new revolutionary technique through automation. We shall soon have the possibility of producing wealth on a scale greater than mankind has yet conceived. I refrain from giving estimates of these possibilities because they may sound fantastic, but in practice the application of a new form of power to a new industrial technique will soon make them appear as cautious understatements.

Yet in normal circumstances the economies of the western countries during the last half century have been unable to organise a market adequate to absorb the production of which existing industries are already capable. Now science, in one of those great forward leaps by which all nature's vital forces operate, is able to increase beyond all previous bounds the means to produce. Without conscious, deliberate, definite market organisation we are lost. The wage-price mechanism is market organisation; it is the means to this end in a free as opposed to a slave economy.

At present the cut-throat competition on world markets with all the small nations trying simultaneously to sell more than they buy in order to achieve the magic of a favourable balance of payments to which their individual economies impel them, is breaking down the present system into a situation as absurd as it is tragic. To take again our prime case of Great Britain, that country is unable to employ the full productive capacity of industries organised on their present limited basis, for fear of upsetting its balance of payments. Directly even the industries operating for the present relatively small market run at full capacity, the import bill becomes too high and buoyant wages begin to cost Britain out of world markets in competition with lower wage systems. So Britain already begins to move towards a semi-siege economy, by holding production down well below its full capacity in order to avoid an exchange crisis. At the same time that she is thus inhibited from running her industrial machine to full capacity, she attempts simultaneously to support a defence force both nuclear and conventional far beyond her individual strength, a welfare state which is relatively a heavier burden than the social services of America, and to act as banker of the whole sterling area with reserves which are quite inadequate even to her own requirements, and which are, therefore, threatened with disaster directly she expands her position beyond the limits of a semi-siege economy. The only future of a Britain in that position directly any form of world depression arrives, will be a movement from a semi-siege to a complete siege economy in order to live at all. And that situation in Britain will only be the most extreme example of the position to which all the divided, isolated countries of Europe will be reduced. It will be a position of complete collapse long before the fifteen years have run which they allow themselves to make the European market, which in reality they will find they cannot make without common government.

The social democratic parties of Europe, headed by the Labour Party of Britain, as usual add nothing but comedy to tragedy. They solemnly propose to build socialism in a small island like Great Britain, while retaining and even exaggerating the present international system of trade which makes the country completely dependent on exports. When great capitalist institutions cannot compete on world markets and yet maintain even the present British standard of life, we are asked in theory to believe that the nationalised institutions of bureaucratic socialism will succeed under competition with all the low-wage systems of the world in raising our standard of life. The state-paid clerks of nationalised industries will indeed have to prove much more efficient than the long experienced managers of competitive capitalism.

In hard practice it is already recognised in the programmes of the Labour Party, and in the speeches of its leaders, that Britain under such conditions will have to live more than ever on a siege economy, and it was a Labour Chancellor who originally invented the beginning of the method. A very large export surplus is demanded from British industries which is to be secured by a system of rigid controls for the purpose of reducing imports and compelling a further expansion of exports; the result will be an inevitable reduction in the British standard of life, because more goods will be sent abroad and less goods will be used at home. All hopes of enabling the British people to consume what they produce is abandoned, if such a thing ever entered the heads of the socialist leaders. Enormous schemes are contemplated for equipping Eastern countries - such conceptions as the Colombo Plan - with the wealth produced by British workers of which Britain must now divest herself.

Thus the socialist parties of the second international, in hard practice, now perform the last role which Karl Marx reserved in his main thesis for a declining capitalism. The surplus wealth must be exported abroad which the low standard of life occasioned by capitalist competition on world markets does not permit the workers to consume at home. Britain must again become the moneylender of the world in the classic fashion of the last phase of capitalism, or at least America must be taught by a socialist government in Britain how to play the role for which Britain now lacks the funds. In the twentieth century America is to perform the world role of nineteenth century capitalism in Britain under the tuition of the British socialist party. Thus Marx will prove right after all, but not quite in the way that was intended. Can confusion of mind and infirmity of character take a great movement any further away from the purpose it was originally meant to serve?

Meantime a grim figure enters the scene of the final comedy, which it will soon turn to tragedy. Soviet Russia takes a hand at the game in order to accelerate the collapse which Marx foresaw, and it will certainly play the game under Marxian rules. As we noticed in Chapter 2, it is the deliberate policy of Russia to quote ten per cent below any Western tender on the key export markets, with the dual object of breaking the economic system of the West, and of obtaining economic and political influence at the decisive points of the world. To this end the tyranny of communism will oblige the Russian people to do without a substantial proportion of their total production, just as they were previously compelled to abstain from consumption in order to provide that pool of resources which made possible Russia's remarkable scientific advance under the leadership of the captured German scientists. In the battle for world markets tyranny can always win, because it can make its people do without more, and put up with more, than any free system. So we are competing under laws already proved to be fatal, within a system already shown to be failing, against an adversary who possesses the means of inevitable victory on the particular battlefield selected.

All these problems which the Soviets will artificially create for us are in addition to the natural problems caused by the arrival of the age of revolutionary power through nuclear fission and revolutionary industrial technique through automation. Is not this the point at which we must move into the twentieth century; leaving behind us the conflicting creeds of the nineteenth century, capitalism and communism? The old capitalism has practically abandoned the fight, and communism seeks only to exploit with tyranny the forces of the new age for purposes of world dominion. None of the old parties have even begun to think about their control in terms of a free system, which aims at human advancement to an ever higher level of existence. And yet the key is now within our grasp, because science with all its hard, dark dangers has brought the glittering gift of a supreme opportunity. Why should we not match science with human organisation, why should we not take firmly into our own grasp the great area of Europe-Africa which contains within it all we can possibly require or desire? Why should we not then organise a market to equal the present and still more the coming power of production?

This requires certainly and inevitably the economic leadership of government and the use of means such as the wage-price mechanism. It is inconceivable that such great forces should simply direct themselves, if left to chance; it is a childish illusion to believe they will. It is equally foolish to believe that we can simultaneously persuade all men everywhere to have the same ideas and to act together in an immediate world organisation. But it is at least possible to persuade the Europeans within the family of Europe to act together in face of a mortal danger, and in so doing to organise for themselves a prosperity and happiness which was inconceivable before the age of science.

This is the moment for great action, because we have both the external stimulus of deadly danger and the internal incentive of immense reward. Russia can be left in peace to develop her own experiment as we shall see in the next chapter, provided we Europeans can be left in freedom and peace to develop our own life. This is not something which it is impossible for us to do. It can clearly be done directly the Europeans decide to do it. If some 300 million Europeans decide to come together and to build a new civilisation, this thing can be done; that is beyond doubt. It is a question of the will, and of the will alone. Shall the civilisation of three thousand years die for lack of will, at the very moment when it faces by far its greatest opportunity? If we die, we deserve to die; this is certain. Let us first make the effort to give Europe the will to live; and to live greatly.

Chapter 4

War and Peace

Suggestion for a World Settlement

THE question of war or peace now is the gravest issue which has ever faced man, because for the first time in history a wrong decision can bring the world to an end. Any sane man in such a situation must desire peace; the only question is how to get it. Peace can, of course, be too dearly bought, just as life itself can be too dearly bought. If the price of peace is slavery, it is no more desirable than life in a condition of continual agony. Again, no sane man would desire either peace or life in such conditions. It is better to die than to live forever in a state of misery and ignominy. This has been the decision of brave men through the ages, and that resolution has been essential to the progress of mankind. The ultimate will to die, rather than to surrender everything of value in life, must ever be present to a great civilisation. Otherwise it is lost.

When we stand on this firm basis, however, it is clear that peace is quite possible between east and west, possible at any time when both sides face the facts and act sanely. One preliminary condition is of course essential, that both sides are ruled by sane men. It is not necessary for them to be good men or honest men, and certainly quite unnecessary that they should agree in all things; it is only necessary for them to be sane. Sanity in this matter simply means recognition of the fact that war in modern conditions can destroy the world. No sane man will take action which will destroy the earth, including himself, his country, his friends, his ideas and creed; in fact, everything for which he cares in life.

The first essential, therefore, is to make it clear that war will certainly destroy the world, by being as well armed as the Soviets until we can get universal disarmament. After that point, wars cannot occur except by accident, and the next step of sane men must be to remove the possibilities of accident. The final action to complete security will be a political settlement based on the simple principle of live and let live, in the tolerable conditions for all which modern science and the available spaces of the earth can now provide in such ample measures. The question now is how these basic principles of plain common sense can be translated into the practical detail of effective political action.

We must certainly always be ready to approach the Russians and negotiate with them; not merely for immediate purposes of human survival but for the continuing necessity of living in the same world. We can approach them with some assurance that their leaders are sane; no more is necessary. We can believe them to be sane because no men could have survived the rigours of their experience without clear heads and strong characters. We may also believe them to be criminals on a scale with few parallels in world history; men who have frequently committed crimes in the calm of peace far surpassing any crimes committed in the heat of war for which Europeans have continued to hang each other long after the event. But all of these things are irrelevant to the decisive issue, whether or not the Soviet leaders are sane. And the answer surely must be that men who have survived their experiences are sane by the one simple test which in this matter alone is relevant: whether or not they are prepared to blow up the world and everything in it, including Russia, communism and themselves.

This would be the act of hysterical madmen, and if the Russian leaders were in that category they would have been dead long ago; Stalin or the system would have seen to that. It is not among the tough and seasoned characters of long adversity that hysteria is likely to be found, but among the pampered favourites of systems with gentler values and smoother criteria of success. The men who have lived contra mundurn, and have survived the high test of the world's disapproval, are less likely to crack into hysteria and to blow up the world in a moment of excitement or petulance than those who have lain always in the silken lap of fortune.

So in dealing with the Bolshevik leaders, we may be reasonably sure that in terms of life and death realities they are sane. They only kill people if the act does not involve their own death. From the solid, practical basis of these realities, we may mount first to security and then to higher things.

If we accept the principle that it is necessary to meet and negotiate with the Russians, for purposes of living in the same world, it surely follows that these meetings must be not occasional but practically continuous. We must get away from the idea that every year or two, a meeting between statesmen of East and West should be arranged with long preparation, and so many precautions against failure that it can scarcely take place at all except to implement decisions already agreed at secret meetings of diplomats.

This idea derives from the view that such a meeting must end in a triumph or a disaster; the triumph being almost complete victory of the western view and the disaster being failure to agree. In real life the complete triumph is unlikely, and the failure to agree is no disaster. The idea that the failure of a conference to secure immediate agreement is a catastrophe, derives in turn from the period when the break-up of an international conference usually ended in a war. This cannot occur now without world destruction. If the Russians had any way to destroy us without being destroyed themselves, they would before now have imposed communism on the world by force in accord with a creed which has always taught that it is not only legitimate to do this but probably necessary.

The break-up of a conference will bring war no closer; on the other hand any measure of success can make war more remote. The real danger today is not war by deliberate action - provided both sides are fully armed - but war by accident. And to meet each other continually and get to know each other, to understand the mind and method of the other side, and generally to know what is going on, should considerably reduce this risk. If the view then be valid, that a row at a conference brings war no nearer, and that success at a conference reduces the risk of war, it is surely clear that the more meetings we have between East and West the better.

All this, of course, does not imply any shadow of trust; that is out of the question between East and West at present, and also quite unnecessary. It is possible to negotiate with people whom you do not trust in the least; that has been done throughout history. It is quite new, this other-worldly idea that you must like and trust a man before you meet him; the realist characters of history would have found it comical. It is possible in any negotiations to maintain the most genial relationships with people you do not trust at all; as in horse coping. Lack of trust does not matter in this affair; it is a quite frequent condition in practical life. Meeting together continually would at least promote confidence to the extent of enabling a more exact estimate of what each will do and will not do. A practical modus vivendi could in this way gradually be worked out.

The rival merits of private and public diplomacy are always much canvassed. After the first world war the American view in favour of public diplomacy prevailed. Now the pendulum has swung far the other way, and it seems to be believed that nothing practical is ever done except in private. I believe, on the contrary, that truth lies between these two extreme views. We should use both methods to the full on the appropriate occasions. Negotiations should always begin in private, and every effort should be used to reach agreement by quiet, reasonable means. If this fails, and it is plain that the other side is just playing the fool to gain time or to avoid a decision for some purposes of their own, we should make it quite clear that if they so continue we will go outside and tell the world the truth. If necessary, rather than accept defeat or frustration on a point where right is on our side, we should then use every instrument of public debate and propaganda. It is not yet realised how powerful these methods can be in the modern world if wielded by competent hands, and how much the communists would fear them.

The Soviets know perfectly well that in the existing or coming military paralysis, the only hope of their world victory lies with their communist parties. If again and again they were worsted in public debate, exposed as hypocrites who talk peace and disarmament while they really menace the one and obstruct the other, their communist parties in every civilised land would find themselves in sore difficulties. At every bench in every factory, at every street corner, in every pub, bistro, and beer house, good communist party workers would find themselves in a hopeless position in an argument with determined opponents, who had followed the public controversy which modern means can bring to the ears of the whole world.

Communism would lose the battle of ideas, and communism as a political force would begin to fade. That is the last risk which the masters of the soviet world can afford to take. So it comes to this: in frequent conferences we should either make progress towards peace and disarmament in private meetings, or destroy the communist political position in public debate. The risk of war would not be increased, because war means mutual destruction, and we should have it already if that were not the fact. So virtually continual conference can bring nothing but good; in fact, the process is necessary to the effective and safer conduct of the modern world.

What then should be the basis of negotiation from the western standpoint? The premises of all negotiation should be that a real danger of world end now exists, but that it is perfectly possible so to arrange the world that each civilisation can have full opportunity to develop in its own way without any form of interference from others. In a situation now recognised to be really dangerous, such a solution must have some attraction for both sides, if it can be found. For the soviet leaders the attraction of security, and the ability to develop their experiment in their own area and in their own way, should be reinforced by their conviction that the rival civilisation will inevitably fail. In their thesis, they will only have to get on with their own work and wait for all other ideas and systems to succumb. If they are sincere Marxists this must be their attitude, and there is every reason to suppose that this is their true position. We on the contrary can accept the challenge of their ideology with confidence, because we are quite certain that they are wrong and that we have a stronger and clearer idea with which we can make a better system and a superior civilisation.

It is only those who have no idea, neither faith nor plan, who cannot face the conflict of rival experiments in human society conducted in separate areas without possibility of interference with each other. Those who reject any such solution, and cling to an uneasy and dangerous status quo, incur a suspicion that they use armament booms on the edge of war to replace the actual wars into which the men of the old world escaped when their systems failed. Such conservative elements confirm the Marxian thesis and thus become its best friend; they make certain of its victory by presenting no alternative, because in the long run of real politics no mere negative can defeat a challenging positive. To defeat communism we need a better system and a stronger faith. It is the task of this book to attempt the description of both.

In the sphere of war and peace we need more than ever a definite and clear cut plan which is deployed in ordered sequence. The idea is entirely wrong that policy should consist simply of finding out what the Soviets want to do and stopping them doing it; a frantic flap round the world to block every move the Russians make. Equally wrong is the concept that policy should consist only of a patchwork of negotiations improvised ad hoc, whenever and wherever trouble breaks out. Simply to oppose whatever the Russians want to do is asking for trouble, and only to negotiate piecemeal when a difficulty has occurred is just following trouble instead of solving problems. These are the methods which have so far been pursued and have failed; they are the devices of the old politics, and the old diplomacy.

It is a serious question we face and without any precedent, this question of whether or not mankind shall survive. It is a great problem and can only be met in a great way. We need above all clear cut design and definite plans. We must begin, of course, with the determination that the Russians cannot simply be allowed to conquer. If we disarmed while the Russians were armed, we would merely present a fanatic with the easy chance of world mastery for his cause. Such a man may be perfectly sane but yet not reject a present of the whole globe to the communist creed in which he believes. If Russia possesses modern weapons while we do not, communist victory is certain. The Soviets would not even have to use the weapons; the threat of their use would be enough, particularly if it were reinforced by the horror propaganda of the Left which is already in full swing.

The classic pacifist position of contentment with unilateral disarmament must face the logical consequences of its attitude in modern conditions; it is the imposition by force of communism on all mankind. No one could possibly expect the soviet leaders in this situation to behave any differently; if they did, they would deny their whole faith and would betray their every principle. Therefore the first element in any clear thinking on the subject must mean that we arm so long as the Russians arm, and at least match them in decisive weapons.

So far that has been the basis of existing western policy, and it is clearly justified in this respect. To the extent that it has failed, there has not been a weakness of intention but a weakness of system accentuated by the incapacity of the leadership which the system produces. We have fallen behind in the race of science, because we have not encouraged science and faced the sacrifice which this entails. Although our resources were far greater, the

Russians have been allowed to get ahead, by reason of their simple resolution to deprive their people of many of the basic necessities of life in order to produce scientists, and to give science the means it needed for rapid development. Not a fraction of that sacrifice would have been needed on our side to outstrip them, but we failed to make the serious effort needed.

It was a failure of character in our rulers and in our system, which had nothing whatever to do with the merits or demerits of communism. Capitalism or any other system in the West could have obtained greater results than the Soviets by devoting to the encouragement of science a lesser proportion of the larger resources available.

But admittedly, to equal or surpass the Soviets in modern weapons is no solution. On the contrary, it creates considerable risk that the start of war by accident can destroy the world. Airborne aircraft carrying live H-bombs, or rockets with H-warheads pointing across frontiers or seas, are liable to all the accidents which can occur in fallible human hands. It is a dangerous and a desperate solution, but it is not so dangerous or so desperate as not being armed while the Russians are armed. In the present situation of each side being armed we risk death; in the alternative situation of only the Russians being armed we should make certain of death or a subjection which would be worse than death. The present solution is thoroughly bad. It has only one merit: all sane men must see that it is too dangerous to leave things where they are, and the very danger of the situation therefore impels a settlement. In our plan, therefore, we must be armed while the Russians are armed, but must press continually for means to remove the danger and secure settlement.

Disarmament is, of course, the most desirable thing on earth. Again any sane man must desire disarmament, but again the practical question is how to get it. This question can only be answered by science. Disarmament becomes practical directly science can provide the means for an effective mutual inspection.

Then it will be clear that each side can be certain the other side is not arming secretly. At this point any statesman capable of a great appeal to the peoples could mobilise the overwhelming public opinion of the world virtually to compel a general disarmament. It would only be necessary for him to publish details of the method whereby mutual inspection could be made effective, and to demand publicly that both sides should disarm completely under these conditions of proved security. If the Russians refused, every communist party outside soviet control would be stricken, and the political battle would be decided by the triumph of the West. And when the means of war become too dangerous for use it is the political battle which will decide all.

The factor now preventing disarmament is the fear that if one side disarms they will then be tricked by an opponent who has pretended to disarm but has really retained the means to destroy them with a surprise attack. The arrival of the missile weapons has made this question particularly difficult, because rocket missiles carrying H-warheads are very easily concealed and can also be very mobile. Disarmament is inevitably held up until science has devised the means for each side to discover whether or not the other side has destroyed its stock of such missiles as well as ceasing to manufacture them. This is really the crux of the whole matter, and all other discussion of the subject is time-wasting verbiage until this single point is settled.

Means to limit conventional forces and to enforce disarmament by mutual inspection were worked out even before the war. That is a far easier problem than disarmament in the sphere of the new weapons, and it was, therefore, more than disingenuous of the Russians so long to emphasise the importance of nuclear disarmament, and to ignore the possibility of disarming the conventional forces in which they possess a decisive advantage. Now that they have a probable equality in the main nuclear weapons, they may well be more ready to make a practical move in the easily feasible reduction of conventional forces to a point where at least neither side can invade other countries with a mass land army.

But the greater cause of present anxiety will remain, until science can invent the means of discovering by mutual inspection whether or not each side has carried out an undertaking to destroy the whole range of nuclear weapons. And when disarmament is represented as something easily obtainable if only everyone would be reasonable, the danger always exists that public opinion in the West will compel it in conditions which are really dangerous. Easy talk of creating an atmosphere of trust, confidence and goodwill can lead to a complete disaster; it is just the chatter that suits a fox which is after a goose. We can take nothing on trust from the Russians, for the simple reason that their creed teaches them that any means are justified to advance their cause, and that they can trick, lie and swindle to any extent for that end. In fact no honest communist will make any concealment at all of that position. So any move to disarm without being completely sure that they will also disarm is just to commit suicide.

It is really incredible that some people are prepared in such life and death matters to take the word of a communist on trust, while they would not dream of taking the word of a business friend on trust, and in the simplest everyday matter insist on a contract. The whole network of contract and ordinary business procedure has been built up in human affairs because mankind has discovered that the word of a great many men cannot be trusted. So a business man of blameless record is asked to sign a contract for a matter of a few pounds, but in international affairs the same people who wisely insist on such prudent procedure in private life will often throw all caution to the winds and be ready to stake their country's life, their own life and everybody else's on the word of a soviet leader whose creed openly proclaims that all means are justified to destroy the opponents of communism. The divorce between private practice and public policy was never more absurd, nor more dangerous. In the matter of disarmament we must insist on a binding contract, which simply means effective power of inspection to be sure that the other side is disarming.

Until we reach this point we must live with the present situation, and neither talk nor tears will change this necessity. But is the existing position so disastrous as hysteria represents, or communist propaganda pretends when it wishes to soften the will of the West? It is certainly less dangerous for both men to have a gun than for only one to have a gun. It is even less dangerous to have the other man's gun pressed against your chest, and your gun pressed against his chest, than to be a sitting target for his shooting or even a running target in the best left foot forward style. We are reaching a point where if either man shoots, the reflex action of the other will pull the trigger and kill him too. And, if we cannot yet attain the great blessing of disarmament, we must ensure that this is always the position. It is an uneasy life, but it is not death.

The dangers of accident are, of course, always present. But it is not really very likely that under all the elaborate and deliberate heirarchy of modern command such accidents will actually occur. They are possible, but improbable. The death of the world in these conditions is even less likely than the death of an individual who always keeps a gun in the room. Yet few fatal accidents occur among the numerous people who live with guns and handle them. Guns can always go off, but public guns, with all the precautions which surround them, are less likely to go off than private guns in happy-go-lucky hands. It is not pleasant for either side to live with globe-destroying rockets pointing in their direction, but so long as it is quite certain that destruction will be mutual, these weapons are not very likely to go off. We often hear of one man shooting and killing another, without injury to himself until the law catches up with him. But we hear of very few shooting matches under conditions in which both combatants are quite certain to be killed. And such an event is even less likely in public than in private life, because the mechanism of destruction is more elaborate and the forces restraining passions are greater. The chances of any of us being run over some evening in the streets of our own city are probably almost as great as our chances of being killed in another war; after all, street accidents are now a considerable risk for everyone.

Let us, therefore, treat the matter as an occasion for thought rather than hysteria; nothing stimulates thinking so much as danger. And this really is an affair which will be settled by thinking rather than by shouting.

Whether or not we get early disarmament, a political settlement will, of course, greatly reduce the dangers of war. It may be optimism at the present stage to believe that complete disarmament is immediately possible, but it is sheer pessimism to believe that a political settlement is impossible. What we need is a clear design, and the capacity to persuade world opinion that it is a solution.

Our first aim must be the entire union of Europe in complete freedom. From this standpoint the most important thing said since the war was the soviet offer at the end of 1956 to withdraw all Russian troops from the occupied lands of Europe, if America would also withdraw her forces from all Europe. This offer was repeated four times during 1957 without response of any kind from western governments. There were no conditions attaching; in fact on two occasions the offer was advanced as a "test" or challenge to see which political system would prove the stronger in free conditions. The failure of the West in general to reply was an extraordinary admission of political weakness because it implied a fear of losing the battle of ideas, and the failure of Europe in particular to reply was a remarkable confession of moral weakness because it implied that nearly 300,000,000 people in a fully liberated Europe could not live without the direct support of America.

After a long interval of silence, western politicians of the left began to move very timidly toward a far more limited plan which asked far less than the Russians had offered. In place of the complete mutual withdrawal by American and Russian forces from Europe, a limited "disengagement" in the central region was suggested. In particular the English Left proposed that all Germany, with the addition of Hungary and Poland, should be a neutralised area in the middle of Europe, between Russia and the American forces which under this plan would continue to occupy the rest of Europe. The soviet propaganda machine quite naturally swung behind the more limited plan, with quick recognition for this gratuitous possibility of getting what they wanted at a lesser price than they had been ready to pay.

From the European standpoint the substitution of the lesser plan for the greater would clearly be a disaster, and it was again quite natural that so many opponents of European union from both Left and Right should support it. For Germany to be left divided from the main body of Europe, which would itself continue to be occupied by American troops, would be a mortal blow for the whole concept of European union. No wonder it was soon welcomed and supported by all enemies of union and by all the interests who benefit from European division. Such elements of course are wont to snatch at immediate advantage for their cause without much thought for the further results; they see the occasion but not the end.

Germany was to be separated from Europe, permitted union at the price of impotence, and mutilated by a perpetual confinement to existing frontiers. No plan could be better devised in the long run to throw Germany into the arms of Russia. An angry and frustrated Germany confined to a small prison in the centre of Europe, severed from all natural affinities in the West and denied the restoration of many of her own peoples, would be under a temptation both to play the old power politics between East and West and finally to join with Russia as the only means of regaining her own people and re-establishing herself as a great power. That is a situation which even the most frivolous Germanophobes of Right and Left in English politics could scarcely view with equanimity.

Contrast this position with the possibility of an entirely united Europe which the larger Russian offer made immediately feasible. The mutual withdrawal of America and Russia from all

European lands would make inevitable a really united Germany, no remaining power could possibly inhibit the force of nature. But it would be a union of Germany within the union of Europe. The west of Germany is already in some degree integrated with the rest of Europe in economic and military matters. It is this fact which makes it such a particularly retrograde step now to suggest the severance of Germany from Europe and the breakdown of the good work of union which has at least begun. Russia might legitimately ask as a condition of withdrawal that no military establishments of any kind should be kept in the liberated territories of Eastern Europe, though no such condition was specifically attached to the offer. But in free conditions nothing in the end could prevent the political and economic union of these lands with the rest of Europe.

The Russians were apparently prepared to submit the matter to the test of freedom, according to their published statement. If they had subsequently withdrawn from that position, once again clear heads and strong voices in the West could have compelled them with a world-wide propaganda either to keep their word or to suffer a disastrous political defeat for communism. The Russians in hard political practice could not then have offered freedom and reappeared as tyrants. But the clear heads and strong voices were lacking to the West. Europe was afraid of greatness.

Yet at any point in the relatively near future when Europe can acquire that quality, the lost opportunity can be restored. A strong western initiative can at any time make it politically impossible for the Russians to resist the mutual withdrawal of American and Russian forces which they have already offered, and finally also the real freedom of all occupied lands. What is it the West fears? Why can it not be done?

The fear can be stated quite shortly: it is the fear of living with the Germans and of living without the Americans. That fear inhibits the making of Europe and compels us to live as divided dependents of America. It is obvious that we cannot make

Europe without the Germans, and if we do not make Europe we all depend on American strength. Britain is faced with the choice between making Europe which includes the Germans or becoming in reality if not in name the 49th State of America. And the other countries of Europe have exactly the same choice, of making Europe or of adding to the number of the American states.

At this point we give a clear decision in the choice between European union and American dependence. We choose Europe. But in so doing we should express our warm gratitude for all America has done and our firm determination to stand shoulder to shoulder with her in an equal comradeship whenever and wherever communism may seek by force to impose its alien creed on the western peoples. We leave ingratitude to the more ignoble members of the considerable political community which seeks for ever to live on American charity without giving anything in return except abuse. Squalid is the dog which bites the hand that feeds.

It is the task of those who believe in the full union of Europe to show how in these circumstances Europe can live. We reply clearly and firmly that in the event of a mutual withdrawal of Russian and American forces, Europe can certainly become a national community which looks after itself, and that science has given it ample means to this end. Nothing is lacking but the will, and necessity can quickly awaken that will. In fact, nothing is more desirable than to confront Europe with the necessity of saving herself, and thus to awaken again the mighty will of the European peoples to live, and live greatly.

None of the questions raised by this situation is insoluble; it is always a simple question of the will to solve them. A good example is the question of European defence in the absence of the Americans. There is something immediately and visibly shameful in the suggestion that nearly 300 million Europeans cannot defend themselves under any conditions against 170 million Russians. But science now provides means to make the task relatively easy; we do not any longer require a great manpower to stop Russian mass. At the time this book is written, intermediate range ballistic missiles exist which from bases in Great Britain could if necessary devastate the whole of Western Russia. A relatively few modern divisions, armed with short-range rockets and A-warheads, could also put down a curtain of fire which would expose Russian mass attack to annihilation. These weapons can be manned by comparatively few specialists; the days of the steamroller, of the overwhelming infantry mass are over for ever.

It would, of course, be far better to accompany the mutual withdrawal of American and Russian forces by a far-reaching measure of universal disarmament. But for reasons already noted it may be impossible at this stage of scientific development to secure an effective mutual inspection of easily concealable rocket weapons, which alone could make such a measure safe for the West. Even so it should be possible to obtain a mutual disarmament of conventional forces, at least to a point which made invasion by either side impossible. And even if we have to live with rockets pointing at each other until science provides the means for a controlled disarmament, such a situation need not be the end of the world, for reasons also already noted.

The point of the matter in this context is that science can easily give a united Europe with a highly skilled and technically gifted population the means to resist any possible Russian attack. We can have the great deterrent just as well as America, the means to ensure the death of both sides in the event of war which is the only relative safety until complete disarmament is possible. In fact, as this book is written we are on the way to obtaining the necessary weapons.

It is, of course, true that America cannot withdraw from advanced European bases and expose herself to bombardment from Russian intercontinental ballistic missiles until she has developed these weapons for purposes of retaliation if that should be necessary. America presumably would not be content to place her life in European hands in the confident manner that Europe has placed her life in American hands for long past. But again, it is only a matter of a very short time before these weapons are ready; negotiation of all the details of withdrawal is likely to take at least as long as their production. The time is not far distant when Europe can have IRBMs with which to hit back at any Russian attack and can also have America in support with ICBMs. Can reliance on force be better sustained, until the happy day when disarmament is possible, and we can rely on something better than force? There is really no reason whatever why Europe should not now do without America. And no one can deny that the withdrawal of both American and Russian forces from Europe would at least reduce the risks of war if Europe remained equally competent to defend herself.

But all of this, of course, predicates a considerable willingness in the European people to unite, even if they are not immediately ready to go so far as Europe a Nation. All problems are progressively improved, and all the risks are reduced, as we approach that point. Take, for instance, the frontier question between Germany and Poland, which would become very acute if the suggestion were adopted to strap Germany up with Poland as two separate countries in a neutral belt in the centre of Europe. If, on the contrary, the occupied countries were evacuated and really free to follow the desires of their peoples, and a popular movement towards union then developed with inevitable and irresistible force throughout Europe, this problem would naturally and easily be resolved within a united Europe. It is obvious to the point of platitude that no frontier question could arise within a really united Europe; such questions could not exist within Europe a Nation.

The union of Germany is naturally and rightly the chief interest of the German people. It should naturally and rightly be of paramount interest to the whole of Europe. These lost lands are European lands; we want them back, and we demand their return. We cannot make a healthy, a prosperous and a happy Europe while limbs are severed from the trunk. We cannot have a war to get them back, because that would mean world destruction. We must use political means to secure their return, but in the coming period political means will be immensely powerful. It is unnecessary to add that the political means available to all Europe for securing the return of the lost lands would be far stronger than those of an individual country, even a nation as strong as Germany is again.

If both America and Russia evacuate all Europe, and East Germany is evacuated in the process, all that we really require is an absolute assurance that neither America nor Russia will return. That assurance will, in fact, rest on the certainty that neither can return without a world explosion which none will dare risk. In that situation the return of the lost lands can be left with calm certainty to the force of nature aided by a strong political pressure.

A Russian demand for the maintenance of no military establishments in Eastern Germany could be easily conceded; they are not necessary in that position if major wars are excluded, and if we are confident of getting what we want by political means. It would also be wise not immediately to raise frontier questions, or even to worry much in the early days about a conflicting political system in East Germany. Once we get rid of the Russians, time, nature and political skill will do the rest. If we can avoid the disaster of war, we shall then win the rest of the hand. And with the instruments of world propaganda in competent grasp we could prevent soviet success by various means of covert force, because any move of that kind could be exposed with deadly effect to their whole political position in the world. Once all Europe is free from outside occupation, the rest will be politics; and we do not fear the battle of ideas. The cause that wins the support of the people will be victorious.

The major question of German union like so many other questions might be settled quickly, provided opinion in Germany strongly supported the movement for complete European union. A great, popular movement throughout all Europe could sweep away all frontiers and submerge all lesser questions. Defence, frontiers, economic difficulties, as we have already seen, all these questions can be resolved in the fiery crucible of the peoples' will to fuse at last our divided countries into a new and greater entity of Europe.

Our first task is to concentrate the will of Europe effectively on what is practical and attainable. For this end it is necessary above all to have a clear design and coherent purpose. We must make up our own minds what to do, before we can ask other people to do anything. In terms of political design this means deciding what Europe wants and does not want; what we must hold and what we can afford to relinquish.

This decision is properly divided into two parts, in chronological order. In the end we shall need nothing more than Europe and white Africa to build our European civilisation. In the interval before we have completed the new system, we shall need some of the old colonial positions for purpose of supply. As already suggested, our difficulties in these matters will be greatly reduced, directly we are capable of explaining what we are doing in a clear plan with a definite and limited objective. The retention of certain positions for the time being will be much easier, if it is made clear what exactly we mean to hold and for how long. Our word in this matter will also be more readily believed when such proposals are part of a clear design to build Europe-Africa in the shortest possible time, and thus to render redundant many of the old colonial positions from which we at present derive primary products. The full plan should be declared at the outset: we mean to build in Europe, white Africa, the British Dominions and such other European overseas territories as care to enter our economy, an economic entity which can be entirely independent of world supplies and the chaos of world markets. In the end we shall need nothing else, and all action outside this area can, therefore, be a matter of temporary expediency until our plans are complete.

Directly we have such clear design, a political settlement with the Soviets on a great scale becomes possible. We should disinterest ourselves entirely in Asia. Our basis of world settlement would be: hold Europe-Africa, leave Asia. We are, in reality, giving away nothing, because the Soviets will certainly have most of Asia in the end unless we fight a catastrophic war to prevent it. Soviet propaganda is probably far better adapted to winning Asiatic peoples to their side, and in some respects at least, their system and method are better suited to the traditional forms of Asiatic development. We cannot win in the East without force, and we are certainly not prepared to use force, to risk the life of Europe and the West for that purpose.

It is better from the outset clearly and courageously to face the plain question: are we prepared to fight a war which can bring the end of mankind in order to save Asia? No sane man in the West would answer that question in the affirmative if he squarely faced it. As we have no other effective means of saving Asia, we had better write Asia off as a military commitment without more waste of time, loss of resources and jeopardy of world settlement. It is a hard decision, but it contains the ultimate reality, and to refuse much longer to face realities can bring world disaster.

This course is merely to recognise the inevitable before it is too late and to concentrate our strength on doing what is possible. The surest way to lose all is to try to do everything. We have quite enough to do in Europe and in Africa with our available strength and resources. And to block every outlet for Soviet development is the quickest way to a world explosion. We can deal with this matter only by a world war which the dangerous force of the new weapons rules out, or by a settlement which means giving the Soviets room to live and develop their own experiment in human society. These matters must be settled: let us have Europe-Africa and let them have Asia.

The question of the American attitude is, of course, something, we cannot settle; we can only give the most friendly advice. It is reasonable to assume that the American citizen and taxpayer will not wish American armies to go plunging for ever about the mainland of Asia in order to prevent by force the spread of the communist doctrine among Eastern peoples; particularly if such local struggles risk the outbreak of world war. In the end America, like Europe, must decide, what it will hold and what it will leave. The only military necessity to America is the chain of islands stretching from Japan through the Philippines to the south-eastern periphery of Asia, which an alliance of mutual interest with Japan and commercial friendship with the island peoples can ensure. Nothing else in Asia is vital to the life of America, except possibly a market which she can find elsewhere.

It is difficult too for America in the name of freedom indefinitely to fight wars to prevent peoples voting communist. For instance would either Britain or America fight a war to prevent India going communist if the Indian people voted communist? The most advanced state in India has already voted communist, and one of the ablest American ambassadors several years ago gave his considered opinion that a fifty-fifty chance existed of India becoming a communist state.

These questions will have to be faced in the end if western powers are not to risk fighting a world war to prevent what they have defined as freedom. Communist propaganda will in the end take Asia from them with the certainty of a hen leading chickens away from a weasel. The clucking may be intelligible to no one but the chickens, and a worried Middle Western conscience may certainly feel it is no weasel, but that is how it will appear to the Oriental and that is certainly what is going to happen. How long is America going to take these risks and spend all this money in defiance of the inevitable?

Sooner or later it will also become clear to the American taxpayer that all these grandiose schemes for the equipment of the East at American expense - in which the British Labour leaders particularly specialise - are simply devices to equip the Soviets, because the countries thus endowed are never grateful to the donor and are very likely in the end to fall into soviet hands. It will then not appear so wise to have used American resources to gild the plums which fall into the soviet mouth. But the Soviets can well afford to delay their harvest until everything possible has been squeezed from the American taxpayer for the future equipment of soviet government.

All of this merely wastes time and resources which are urgently needed in Western lands, and postpones rather than accelerates the hour of final settlement. It is time that we curtailed the merriment of the Soviets at our universal charity, and formulated a clear design with defined and limited objectives. The soviet leaders of course believe that the West is incapable of doing this, because in their theory capitalism cannot survive unless it discards a substantial proportion of its total production in equipping other countries by loan or charity. We have already suggested the European answer to the classic Marxian dilemmas in Chapter 3, and the same solution is of course available to America. But if America persists in her present ways, it is still not necessary to fall into the Soviet trap of equipping future communist territories in the desire to discard the surplus wealth of the American economy, and in the vain hope of forestalling and frustrating the political victory of the Soviets in Asia.

Cannot all of us in the West decide with clarity exactly what we will do, instead of muddling along in the present patchwork fashion? We Europeans will have plenty to do in developing Europe-Africa. We shall have no need to discard any part of our total production, because we know the means to enable our own people to enjoy it, and we shall need too much of our production for a time to develop our food and raw material resources in white Africa. Also one of the tragic paradoxes of the age is that great regions in European countries - Southern Italy for one example, much of Spain for another - live today in direst want, for lack of the capital equipment which is showered from Europe and America on Eastern peoples who often have not the least idea how to use it. What are called the "poor five" countries of Europe: Ireland, Portugal, Greece, Turkey and Iceland, are held back from the development which could be rapid for lack of the capital which is always available for the political game we are losing in the Far East. Much development capital will also be needed to open the French oil supplies in the Sahara and other African regions, which can render us independent of precarious supplies from America and the Middle East. The list of capital required in Europe for essential development is very long; even if you retain the tact not to suggest to the long indoctrinated English that the clearance of slums in British cities, which still disgrace our civilisation, need not by any law of nature rank lower down the queue of applicants than the latest development of local amenities by the present government of Ghana. In short, all our European resources can be adequately employed in Europe, white Africa and our related overseas territories.

But if America is looking for a job and some outlet for her surplus production, because she has not learnt how to solve the Marxian dilemma, why not let her take over the economic development of black Africa? We Europeans during recent years have made rather a mess of some of our colonial positions, and have thereby incurred many reproofs from America. Since we need all our resources for our own purposes, why not allow America to employ both her surplus of wealth and of emotion, to develop the old colonial positions in Africa which have a black population? This would solve the problem of American surplus and of negro poverty. The development of the black way of life for a long time to come will also probably need some white guidance as well as white assistance. It would perhaps be better to use Americans from the northern rather than the southern states for this charitable task. Also it should be remembered that some American doctrines on the basic freedoms might not be immediately understood by those who celebrated their freedom from the often-denounced British tyranny by at once establishing concentration camps for their political opponents. But all this need not any longer be our business.

Would Britain lose anything except the obligation to repay the sterling balances, which in total would completely bankrupt our present island economy? No one should delude himself that Britain could long continue to sell colonial products for dollars, and make payment to the producers in more or less blocked sterling, once these colonies have realised their new independence. And would Europe lose anything in territories which in the past may have afforded some advantage, but in the future can be nothing but a burden for generations to come? America, on the other hand, would find an outlet for her resources and her energies, which is at present indispensable. Europe would at last be off her hands, and in grateful recognition of past kindnesses would wish her well and hand her a most substantial portion of the white man's burden.

This plan of world settlement can also find full occupation for the Soviets. They would, in any case, have much of Asia on their hands, and that problem would keep them busy for generations. They would be obliged to find from their production a bigger surplus for this purpose than Marx ever observed in capitalist economies during his most perspicuous researches. If they failed to do enough, they would politically be most discredited. The whole economic effort of the Soviets, both in Russia and in China, would be diverted to showing what they could do in the constructive task of developing Asia, rather than to disturbing the rest of the world. Their work in Asia would be so big that they would not have enough resources for both, and if they did not perform that duty their creed everywhere would suffer a decisive reverse. Nothing is more satisfactory than giving a man who has long told everyone how to do it, a chance to do the job himself; it is the quickest and best way to deal with a nuisance if the process is not too expensive.

In this case the procedure would be pure gain for the West. We should be relieved of present pressure and any errors the Soviets might make would be at their own expense. At length the self-appointed champions of the underdog the whole world over, would have a chance to do something practical for the poorest and neediest of the underdogs on their own doorstep. And their system would be judged by the results. In fact under these conditions the future would finally be settled by world judgment of rival political ideas, clearly expressed in easily comparable systems. Only those who have neither idea nor energy need fear the results.

It should be observed that this suggestion is not just a cynical cession of Asia to the Soviets in order to relieve ourselves, and to exhibit soviet failure at the expense of the poor Asians. There is no reason at all why the Soviets should not succeed in this respect, and we will genuinely wish them well. In many ways their idea and their method are better suited to the rapid advance of very backward populations than the higher idea and more civilised method which will be born in the west. The conscience of the European is probably too sensitive in very primitive conditions, and he is inhibited by a traditional conduct of which the East knows nothing. In India for instance, in the last days of the British Raj, it was quite evident that a far stronger hand was necessary to get the urgently needed economic results than British parliamentary democracy could possibly supply. The hereditary system, with its tendency to split agricultural holdings into ever-smaller allotments, was so defined by religious beliefs and had to be sacrosanct to us. But it was entirely inhibitive of the basic measures needed to prevent recurrent famine, which modern science could easily provide. The Soviets will have no such inhibitions.

The departure of India in economic terms, would merely free us from onerous obligations and release resources for building our own civilisation. We should not need an Indian market when we have a market of three hundred million Europeans and all of white Africa. Serious consideration of outlying markets only arises in the chaos of present conditions.

On the other hand, it must be affirmed that any loss of Indian culture and religion in its higher aspects, would be a real disaster to world civilisation. The full moral force of the West should be used in their defence, but not the physical force (the Indian leaders should welcome this, because they believe only in moral force, outside Kashmir); we cannot defend everything everywhere, and we cannot block soviet development everywhere without explosion. But moral force in such spheres is something not lightly to be dismissed. Even if the Soviets ultimately possessed India in the physical sense, the spiritual heritage of India must be preserved in a peaceful settlement of the world. The Soviets will not want to appear as the universal barbarian (great performers tire eventually of the old roles), and the moral appeal of the West, reinforced by a really vigorous world propaganda, may yet save many old cultures which come under their sway.

Also, if the present government in India and in smaller lands can make good with their economic measures, it is extremely unlikely that they will be disturbed by the Soviets, even in the absence of any European or American military guarantees. The Soviets will prefer to wait, particularly in the east, until the economic collapse of their opponents, which they regard as certain, shall bring them political victory. The marching of armies will become too dangerous in future conditions for reasons already noted. Shooting anywhere may always start shooting everywhere, and will not be worth the risk.

In military matters we are approaching the age of the "paralysed giants" as I described it in 1950 in The European Situation. This will be a period in which neither side will dare to use its main forces for fear of world destruction, but which will be marked by an intensive political struggle under cover of the mutual paralysis. The Soviets will reckon to win throughout the East by economic and political means, and unless oriental governments can find a higher ideal and a stronger system suited to their own civilisation, the soviet calculation will quite soon prove to be correct.

We shall then be faced with the decisive question already stated: are we prepared to release world war in order to prevent the political victory of communism in Asia? We all know perfectly well that when it comes to the point, we shall not be prepared to do this. It is better, therefore, to free our minds of inhibiting illusions, to clarify our policies and to prepare a great design of world settlement which would enable us to get on with our real task of building in Europe-Africa the highest civilisation the world has yet seen.

What is the alternative for Britain? Do we prefer to stay outside Europe and to tie ourselves to the remnants of the coloured Commonwealth in the nostalgic illusion that it is still an Empire? Are we going to strap ourselves up to the black colonies in a three-legged race against the full strength of a united Europe, a united soviet system in Russia and China which is ready to work everywhere for our destruction, and the full power of America driven to the extremes of competition on world markets because it has no other outlet? Are we to find in addition a perpetual surplus in our balance of payments by open competition on world markets, for the purpose of supplying modern capital equipment to all the primitive peoples of our most backward colonies?

Are we also to make multiple contribution to the worldwide network of alliances necessary to protect them? The whole concept is the most childish nonsense in present conditions, a hangover from a truly remote past in minds insufficiently developed to comprehend the present. Everyone capable of thought knows this to be true, directly he has the courage to face the facts. The situation is too serious to live in a dream; Britain must awake.

Opponents will reply that this plan is fantasy because it is too big. We answer that the fantasy of today is often the obvious of tomorrow, and the platitude of the day after. Let those who say it cannot be done, at least explain what they think can be done. So far they have contributed nothing but confusion; a muddled improvisation which is dangerous because it has no design, and no one therefore can understand their purpose. We have clear design and firm purpose, which can be simply and shortly stated. We shall have Europe-Africa: the Soviets will have Asia. We do not any longer fear their quantity, because in conditions of modern science the world will be determined by quality. The Soviets can find both their outlet and the testing of their system by the development of Asia. America can find an outlet and a mission in the development of black Africa.

The U.S. will meet Europe in South America, which is a heritage of both. British Dominions which hesitate to enter European economy should remember that their places can all too easily be taken by South American countries which are seeking a market for the same products. They should not hesitate too long, though, as we shall observe in a later chapter, the link between a hesitant Dominion and the mother country can still be preserved by the beneficent influence of the Crown. Europe and the Soviets will meet in the Arab lands, which are the natural geographic link between us. We shall need nothing from the Arab countries once we have developed our own oil resources in Africa, and possibly in South America, except a secure bridge in North Africa between Europe and the main primary resources of Africa. This should present no considerable difficulty once new ideas and new men have surpassed the bitterness of past errors, and have re-established a natural friendship between European and Arab which should never have been broken. That friendship is now reinforced by the common interest of preventing the universal triumph of communism.

Europe will then quite simply be able to get on with its own business. What is the business of Europe? To solve our present economic problems which are proving insuperable to the divided states, struggling for life on world markets between the rival giants. To avert the final disaster, the fatal recurrence of history which would destroy us, just as the related states of classic Greece perished when they fought each other and failed to unite in face of the barbarian. Beyond these prime necessities, to be free from all preoccupations except to build the highest form of civilisation which mankind has yet seen. To this end we need nothing except the means of life: food, raw materials and space enough to build our system in freedom and independence of present world chaos.

We need nothing more; let others do the things which we have done for generations but which now distract us from our real task. We have gone beyond all that, but they have not yet. We can find the means of a higher life which they will only find later. Our duty is now to show the world how great a civilisation can be created with the aid of this new genius of science. This is our mission, and we need no other. Let the Europeans unite, and then do this best thing.

Chapter 5

European Government

Structure and Method

THE question of power is not easy, but it has to be settled. It is not easy because it encounters a conflict between two necessities; the need for life to continue, and the need for liberty if life is to be happy or even tolerable. It has to be settled, because in modern conditions life cannot continue without some exercise of power; the reason is that existence has become too complex. We are beyond the period when things could be left to chance, to the free play of natural forces. Such forces of nature are now released that their free play can only mean destruction. Either we must control them or they will destroy us. That is why power must be used somewhere, by some men under some conditions. It is no longer something that we can simply do without. And like many other things, we are now compelled to use power long before men are really fit for it. The study of making men fit for power has not advanced since Plato addressed to it his extraordinary intellect two thousand three hundred years ago, but the problem has now become very acute, most urgent.

Can we then devise a system whereby the need for the use of power can be combined with the other need for preserving in full measure the basic individual freedom? The modern world has been rent by the quarrel of those who attach more importance to one or the other of these two necessities. Cannot we now find a synthesis of these opposing opinions at the higher level of a new civilisation?

It is no good any longer just saying: we have had the fight between authority and liberty, and it is over because liberty has won. Even if that view of the matter were valid, the further question now arises - what the victorious principle has done with the world, and what chance mankind has of long survival under present methods. We have all been made very familiar in recent times with the argument against authority, it is based on much experience and many errors committed by those in authority. We are at present being made equally familiar with the argument against what is now miscalled liberty; it is also becoming well-founded on errors which are already very visible and on an experience which may soon be very painful.

Those who stood for action to enable life not only to continue but to advance, and also to give their peoples a better life by reason of that action, made errors which resulted in the destruction of their system and of themselves. But those who stood against any such principle of action, in the name of liberty and the paramount interest of the individual, have subsequently also made errors which are clearly threatening the destruction of their system, even if so far they have brought no harm upon themselves. In short, we have experienced the fatality of dynamism; we are now beginning to experience the fatality of lethargy. Neither the exaggeration of the need for action in the interest of the whole and of a coherent life purpose, nor the exaggeration of the need for liberty to the point of setting individual interest above the whole, and of paralysing all effective organisation of life, has worked out very well in practice. The one ended in sudden death; the other looks like ending in slow death, if it does not drift aimlessly to the point of a finally fatal explosion which is now possible.

Liberty is important; of course, it is immensely important. No one need be surprised at the constant emphasis on the necessity of a free system in these pages. This is no attitude born of some trivial expediency; it is derived from a deep experience and exceptional opportunity of observing the way of men in practical life. Nothing but liberty will work in the end. Liberty is no joke; it is a basic need. But neither is chaos a joke; it is no joke because in present conditions chaos can mean the death of all. Without organisation on a great scale chaos will come, and organisation means action, vigour, decision, coherent purpose in life; all those things which some have come to believe are the enemies of liberty.

So we come back to our root problem, how to combine action with liberty, how to make the great synthesis. Simplify and synthesise; the capacity to do these two things is the real test of intellect in the modern age. Let us at least attempt in this supremely difficult problem to do both. We can, in any case, begin with an initial simplicity. We need both action and liberty; experience shows that we cannot do without either. Until a very short time ago we could have done without action, at least on any great scale. Until the last century action was seldom really a need; it was far more often the urge of some brute or busybody to impose his will on other people. What was needed was much more of the principle: live and let live. And this is always a very desirable principle; if it be not now exaggerated to a point of letting individuals live for a little and the civilisation die for good.

Action is now necessary because life has become so complicated that existence cannot continue without it. Too late now to take the decision to leave things alone. If that was the desirable way to live, men should have taken the decision long ago to live like Ghandi with his spinning wheel and simple needs, and to forbid the development of modern science. But for better or worse we have got beyond that situation. To use a metaphor I have employed before, we are now in the position of passengers in an aeroplane at a very great height from the ground. There was a strong argument against ever going up in an aircraft at all. But there is no argument now for strapping up the pilot and letting the aircraft land itself. No matter if the machine is in difficulties, no matter if we believe the pilot to be very incapable, no matter if we can cite numerous cases of pilots crashing aeroplanes and killing all the passengers, there is now no argument for leaving the landing of that aeroplane to chance; for better or worse we have to give some pilot authority to do the best he can. But all these reflections do not inhibit us from discovering how to make better aeroplanes and to train better pilots; on the contrary, once you have begun the business, the only course is to continue and make a good job of it. There is much to be said against making this complex modern civilisation, but now we are in it we have to recognise that power exercised by some people, somewhere, is necessary. Our task is not to destroy power, but to make men fit to use it and, in the meantime, to make a system which they can work by methods that ensure the minimum danger and inconvenience to their fellows.

When we reduce these broad principles to the practical, they mean that we require two things: a strong executive, and the means to change the executive easily and rapidly if it fails or abuses power. These two necessities are not easy to combine, but the synthesis is quite possible. We need not lose much time in discussing the danger of dictatorship, because anything of the kind is clearly out of the question in an organism so large and so complex as Europe a Nation, or any form of complete union of the European peoples. Before the war I suggested a more authoritative system of government than I am here recommending in the light of subsequent experience and reflection, though it certainly could not be described as dictatorship because it retained the right of the people to dismiss the Government by free vote at regular intervals. It is also profitless now to discuss whether any great nation of the West could, in fact, be compelled to do what it did not wish to do by any person who could properly be described as a dictator. These questions are now matters for history, and can be dealt with as history at the right time.

It is at least clear in the future which we are now discussing, that no single man could be selected from one of the nations of Europe and set up as any kind of dictator over a whole which comprised all the peoples of Europe. No one would put up with it for a moment, and any such idea is out of the question. Any form of European government must be a team, or an equipe, drawn from all the European peoples; a team of equals. And it is also clear to anyone who reflects at all on the problems involved, that any European government must be entirely subject to the will of the people, chosen by their free votes at free elections which any party may enter, and subject to dismissal by a vote which is equally free to choose another government. Liberty is necessary in the new Europe not only because it is in itself desirable, but because nothing else will work. The relevant question is how to reconcile that liberty with the necessity for action, without which the will of the people cannot be carried out, and without which, too, in the complexity of modern conditions life itself cannot continue. For this purpose let us first consider the necessary character of a strong executive, and then study the checks and controls which can prevent the abuse of power and preserve liberty in all its forms, both public and private.

The executive we desire must be free to act without loss of time, because in modern conditions it is dangerous for a government to lose time. Delay may now mean not merely inconvenience, dislocation, wastage, suffering as in the past, but destruction and death. And that disaster can come, not only through war, which will ultimately be rendered less likely by the march of science for reasons which we discussed in Chapter 4, but through the rapid development, the almost lightning changes of the economic situation which the march of science on the contrary is now likely continually to accelerate. Even if economic events did not in their own natural course constantly require the rapid action of government, the continual and malevolent pressure of a rival and hostile system would compel it. In short, if we are to match events and to outstrip the competitive system, we must have a government which is capable of rapid action while preserving every principle of liberty.

It seems quite clear from results that neither the present American method nor any of the various methods presently employed by the main European nations is entirely adequate to the rapid action which is necessary for the making and the maintenance of the new Europe. It can, of course, be replied that the faults which are so obvious in present failures are not due to anything inherent in the method of government but to the fact that none of the individual European nations has space or means enough to work out any real economic policy for reasons already given, and that America has not yet found it necessary to get round to thinking about a real, coherent economic policy at all. And there is a great deal in these arguments, though they are no final answer. They could only be accepted as a complete reply, if it was clear that the methods in question could be used for action with sufficient decision and speed when a real economic policy was adopted. Could, for instance, the exact method of government prevailing either in America or in the various European countries of today, implement with sufficient speed any economic policy necessary to the rapid construction of the new Europe in a period of crisis?

It is surely clear that in such circumstances they are both far too slow-moving to be effective. Cannot we, therefore, devise a method of far more rapid action while preserving the essential principles of the western democratic system? The delays of the present British parliamentary system are admitted to be irksome even in the running of a small island and the maintenance of effective contact with its self-governing Dominions and Colonies, while few Frenchmen would claim that the present method of the French Parliament would be entirely adequate to the rapid construction of a new continent. The American method can lead also to a conflict between executive and legislature and may result in complete paralysis during a critical period. It can also be very slow-moving. So we must seek a method which provides for rapid action, and yet preserves the liberties which these systems enshrine. I believe the answer can be found in a return to the first principles of all effective organisation: clear division and definition of function.

There are, of course, many different ways in which duties may be divided and defined. I will here suggest methods which appeal to me, but there are many others. All I ask in principle is recognition of the essential method of clearly dividing and defining function, as the basis of all successful organisation. Let all know what they have to do, and let them be held responsible for how they do it. It is a principle which every practical man can recognise as effective in the simple terms: give a man a job to do, judge him by the results, and sack him if he makes a mess of it. I suggest that in principle the method of government can be reduced to a similar, effective simplicity. The making of Europe gives a good opportunity for a fresh start on lines which are possibly new in some respects to western governments, but are already well-proven in the practice of daily life.

It is now necessary to consider how function should be divided and defined between executive, legislature and judiciary. I suggest that government should be entirely responsible for foreign affairs, defence, order, science, and economic leadership by methods already described in the determining of wages and prices. It should also have power to initiate legislation in Parliament. The revolutionary principle in this suggestion is, of course, that government should be solely responsible for finance, subject to certain checks on abuses which we will shortly consider. Foreign affairs, defence and order for all practical purposes are in the hands of government already, and I shall shortly suggest certain safeguards against abuse of the powers relating to order which at any rate do not exist in Great Britain today. The new principle of government determining wages and prices has already been discussed at length.

Let us now consider the admittedly new concept in Western countries that government should have sole power and responsibility in the sphere of finance. Is Parliament's alleged supervision of finance anything but an almost complete waste of time, since budgets became so large and complex that it is really quite impossible for a legislative assembly of several hundred people to consider them in detail? Yet the solemn pretence that this capacity still exists occupies each year months of parliamentary and ministerial time, in fact, exhausts time and energy which ministers should be giving to their administrative duties. Once a machine has grown so big that it is difficult even for able men with their whole time available to keep on top of their jobs, does any effective means still exist to judge their work and enable the electorate to dismiss them if they do it badly, except the general consequences of that work which every man may judge for himself in the state of the nation and in the condition of his daily life. Cannot the plain truth at last be admitted that government must be responsible for all economic and consequently for all financial matters in the complexities of the modern nation, and that if it be responsible, it must have the power to act, subject always to the right of the electorate to dismiss it if the action is a failure? If we recognise the necessity for economic leadership by government we must also surely recognise the necessity for fiscal decision; economics and finance have clearly too close a relation to permit their separation.

This is certainly a subject on which all must soon make up their minds. Is the great network of power which comprises economics, finance, and, also, certainly science, to be entrusted to government or not? If it is not to be entrusted to someone, somewhere, who has the power of rapid decision, how can it possibly be conducted at all in modern conditions? And who can that someone possibly be, except a government elected by the people? If we are then led to this conclusion - and surely all will be driven to it in due course by the logic of events - the question is on what terms and under what conditions such power should be entrusted to government.

If we recognise the necessity for rapid action and for clean-cut, fearless decision by government in the coming period, it is necessary to make government dependent on the direct vote of the people and not on the vote of the legislature. This is, of course, already the principle in America; the difference between these proposals and the American principle is that we divide function more clearly between executive and legislature, and, in some respects, particularly in the sphere of finance, give the executive more power. But there is nothing novel to western life in the concept of making the life of a government directly dependent on the vote of the people and not on the legislature. I would accordingly suggest that the government be elected every four years by secret ballot on universal suffrage, in an election which any party might enter; an election which would in every way be free. The electorate would then be able to judge the work of the government directly, by result and by observation, and could dispense with the additional assistance of parliamentary debates on such subjects as finance, in the hopes that the time saved would enable ministers to do their jobs better. Such in brief, is the power, responsibility and method I would suggest for the executive.

Parliament would be responsible for all social questions; in fact for everything outside the defined sphere of government. This power would rest entirely with parliament, subject to two powers of government: the first to initiate legislation, which parliament could amend or reject, the second to refuse to finance legislation passed by parliament, this would, of course, in many cases bring it to a standstill. The last reservation of decision to government may be regarded as reducing parliament to impotence in any legislation requiring finance. But, in fact, parliament would have a very effective redress in debating and publicising the matter. If the case of the government were weak, and it failed effectively to defend itself, the attack of parliament would be a big factor in securing its defeat at the next election; a consideration so powerful that no government could ignore it. Parliament would by no means be impotent, even in financial matters.

Parliament would in all other matters be very powerful, not only in the passing of legislation, but in the review of grievance and the maintenance of liberty. I would certainly suggest that ministers be subject to parliamentary questions for a good number of hours each week. It would do no minister anything but good to have to attend parliament for his personal interrogation during at least one full hour each week. Only a capable man could stand up to it, and no others are needed. Not only would the process be good for ministers, but it would discover new talents for the service of the nation among the questioners.

There would be every advantage if, in addition to debating legislation, parliament should on a reasonable number of occasions debate both the redress of abuses and major creative principles. Again, one of the main purposes of parliament would be served on such occasions, because they would enable new talent to be discovered. The rising young man would have opportunity to deploy his ability on great occasions when parliamentary time was no longer encumbered by the trivial, instead of scrambling through a few minutes of small committee points at rare intervals, while all major occasions were reserved for the established great. We must always preserve not only existing means of finding new men, but continually seek to devise fresh means. The difficulty of lifting new talent from beneath the machine of the system is the nightmare of any able and enlightened man working a totalitarian method, and the same difficulty is being created by the rigid machine of modern Parliament which is caught fast in a detail that excludes big opportunities for new men. Parliament should not only be the sounding-board of a nation, but the laboratory of new ability.

The question arises how parliament should be elected; and the answer does not really affect the main principles suggested in this book. So long as functions are clearly divided and defined, and the executive has adequate power of action during its term of office, it would certainly not adversely affect the working of the system proposed if parliament were elected on a geographical basis as at present, either by the single constituency method of Britain, or by the proportional method more prevalent in other European countries. I would personally prefer an occupational to a geographical franchise, but it is not essential to the system of government proposed. The advantage of the occupational method of voting is that it should add seriousness to parliamentary discussion, and in a very serious age it is an advantage to have a serious parliament. If men and women were elected by their fellows in their various industries and professions, they would come to parliament as farmers, or farmworkers, as engineers, as chemists, as textile workers, etc.: not as the representatives of some particular residential area, whose inhabitants have little more in common than the accident of residence which, in this unfortunately rootless epoch, is often quite fortuitous. They would be elected by people with whom they had a real community of interest, and would, therefore, be likely to be among the most competent people in their various callings and have come to parliament for the serious purpose of discussing matters they very thoroughly understood. The extremes of partisanship in such conditions would surely yield to the more judicial atmosphere of people earnestly seeking truth in an assembly which would pool the abilities of the nation.

Also if we accept the premise that the decisive sphere is now economics, it seems a reasonable conclusion that the legislature should emerge from this region of reality as a result of election on an industrial and occupational franchise, rather than on a geographical franchise which was originally intended to represent a particular agricultural area but now represents nothing in particular, since agriculture long ago ceased to be the only industry, except in certain purely rural areas which would in any case have their own agricultural representatives.

If it be held that a chamber elected on an occupational franchise would be altogether too specialised, it could easily be coupled with a second chamber composed of men and women who had occupied prominent positions in the service of the state, representatives of education, religion, literature, the arts, etc. Science must naturally be prominently represented in both assemblies; in its more technical aspects in the occupationally elected chamber and in its broader aspects of pure research in the second chamber which would be occupied with more general subjects. But these are issues which are not germane to the main subjects here discussed.

All such matters will have to be settled in detail by the first assembly which is elected on universal franchise by the European people, when the peoples of the present individual nations exercise their existing national franchise in favour of a government which stands for full entry into Europe. Such an assembly would naturally be charged with the task not only of settling relatively minor matters concerning methods of franchise and voting, but of deciding the larger constitutional questions which have been discussed above. And the controversy preceding the election of that assembly would doubtless deal in acute fashion with many and conflicting proposals. A book of this kind can only in general outline suggest one set of principles. They will no doubt be challenged by many other and opposing principles. These issues can in the end only be settled by an assembly of Europe elected to make a constitution. It could, of course, be composed of delegates from each of the national parliaments which have decided to enter Europe, or of delegates from the governments concerned. But it would surely be best to bring in the people at once, to divide Europe for this particular purpose into large geographical constituencies and to allow each constituency to elect any European it liked. Sacred simplicity, what is better?

This actual making of the European constitution presents much difficulty to some minds. In practice, I believe, in a period of crisis many of these imagined impediments will quickly disappear. If one great people votes decisively for a government which stands for full and complete entry into Europe, this will bring matters to a head. In a period of crisis, when it gradually becomes clear that no other way out of mounting and menacing difficulties is possible, other great peoples will soon give similar votes. Very soon a sufficient weight of decision will be accumulated to make Europe. If one, two or three of the great countries had so voted, other governments which stood on the brink would be pulled in. When necessity urges because there is only one exit from a burning house into a safer and a wider life, things can happen very quickly. If the idea already exists, it can be swept to the point of reality by a great wave of mass enthusiasm in all the

European countries when we reach the hour of decision. When sufficient governments are elected in a number of countries to make Europe, the people of Europe must be given a chance of the widest, freest and most direct franchise to elect their assembly to make the constitution. In the end it will happen, suddenly and simply, as all great things happen when their time comes; and time comes when it must, not before. What matters then is to be ready with clear ideas, and consequently with the firm decisions which can only rest on clarity and precision of mind. So at this point, we will not return to the reasons for believing that such an impelling crisis will come - those reasons were discussed in earlier chapter - but will rather advance to a closer consideration of the ideas we shall desire to suggest for the decision of the European people when that time comes.

In the structure of government the essential principle I desire to advocate is the clear division and definition of function between executive, legislature and judiciary. Some outline of the respective spheres of executive and legislature have already been suggested. It remains to consider the function of the judiciary, which in these proposals would be much extended. The normal duties of the judiciary would naturally be preserved; in this case, they would be to interpret the laws passed by executive and parliament in their respective spheres. In addition, I would propose that a constitutional duty be vested in the judiciary to release forthwith any person imprisoned without trial, and to quash any retrospective legislation. Surely the very basis of freedom, the first human right, is no imprisonment without trial, and, also, no imprisonment on account of an act which was legal at the time it was done. Yet this basic liberty is often denied at present by those who speak most of freedom. It should be secured beyond all doubt in the new Europe.

There should be no power of executive or parliament to suspend the provision for preventing imprisonment without trial; as the Habeas Corpus Act is often suspended in Britain on the occasions when it is really needed, namely, in times of popular fear and fury, which can be exploited by unscrupulous governments for purposes both of repression and revenge. Retrospective legislation, too, is one of the vilest instruments in the hands of a corrupt executive. If such power is ever admitted, it can be used to punish or penalise a man years later for doing what was perfectly legal at the time it was done. None is safe under such law; it is only necessary for the executive to find out what an opponent did some time back, and subsequently to declare it to be retrospectively illegal, or at least an act which in time of panic enables him to be imprisoned without trial. Such practices must surely end in the new Europe, if liberty is to be embodied in anything nobler than a shady farce.

So far the duties suggested for the judiciary reside in the region of the conventional, if not entirely in the sphere of practice within present Europe. But I wish now to propose a new duty for what must necessarily be a new branch of the judiciary, in performing more effectively and impartially a role previously assigned to parliament; namely the supervision of finance. For reasons already considered, it is in reality impossible for any outside body to exercise effective control over the immense and complex machinery of the modern budget. But it should be possible to give a branch of the judiciary effective power of probing sufficiently to expose corruption or to uncover flagrant examples of waste and inefficiency.

In such event it would recreate confusion of function if the judiciary were itself then given the power to act and to remedy the abuse. In all such cases, its duty must, therefore, be confined to exposing the facts; a very powerful weapon indeed in the modern state and one which, in this case, the executive would much fear. The right, of course, must rest with the executive to reply to the published facts. If the answer failed to convince the people, the fortunes of the government would be most adversely affected at the next election. In fact, a government would be much more damaged by such a judicial report than by a parliamentary attack of political opponents; it would be a very strong check indeed on corruption, abuse and waste.

On the other hand the procedure of publishing such facts would not be used lightly or in a partisan spirit by judges, whatever their political views. For apart from a traditional probity, it would be dangerous to attack without good reason members of an executive who would naturally be skilled in the arts of popular controversy; the result might well be to make the judiciary look silly, and most judges understand very well that it is part of their business to avoid looking foolish. New powers for the judiciary in such matters will be a well-balanced restraint of abuse and check on inefficiency of the executive, which would add equilibrium, confidence and dignity to the state.

Yet another task, I would suggest, should be added to the function of the judiciary, which is entirely novel and would certainly require not only a new branch of the judiciary but, to some extent, a new habit of mind. The development of new ideas in every sphere of national life is not only essential to progress, but in these days can even be important to survival. The apprehension of the able and dynamic executive, is always that new ideas and new men are being suppressed. He cannot, naturally, himself, examine all new ideas and meet all new men: it is necessary always to wade through dross to find the gem, and to meet many a dunce for every genius. There must be some machinery of the state whereby new methods are sifted and new men of talent are discovered and promoted. This grave matter cannot be left to a bureaucracy, which always tends to resist something involving extra trouble, as the implementing of new ideas always does; it is only among the exceptional men in the higher ranges of a great civil service that the qualities of imagination and drive are to be found, and these few are so invariably overworked that they cannot be used for these purposes.

We really need a new machinery to discover new ideas, and to rescue remarkable young men from beneath the cold repression of mediocrity before they become discouraged. To this end I would suggest a new branch of the judiciary, which is charged with examining new ideas in a judicial atmosphere. The procedure would be much closer to that of a law court than of a popular assembly. In a previous book I suggested for such a purpose, a proposer, an opposer and an assessor. The duty of the proposer would be to advocate the new idea as a barrister does in a court of law, the duty of the opposer would be to submit it to a most meticulous and destructive cross-examination; the two advocates would state the pros and cons to the best of their ability, and the assessor would sum up in the manner of a judge and present a well-balanced report to the executive. For again, we must not confuse function; it would not be the business of the judiciary to decide whether the idea should be adopted, but only to make a recommendation to the executive.

In this sphere again, the judiciary should have the power to publish all the facts, if the executive refused to accept an affirmative recommendation and to act accordingly, and also if the executive implemented a proposal despite adverse advice from the assessor. The executive would naturally retain the right of reply. A powerful machinery of the state would thus be at the disposal of new men who have practical new ideas. And an executive would find itself in difficulty if by reasons of fatigue in office or natural inertia, an impression was created by continuous adverse reports to the public by the judiciary that it was opposed to new ideas and lacked the dynamism which the age required.

It is true that in the judiciary itself a new sense of service to a continuing and persisting dynamism of the State would be needed to replace in this new branch of judicial procedure the very natural tendency towards a sense of the necessity to preserve a well-established status quo which exists at present. But the exigencies of the new age, and a new concept not only of the State but of the purpose of human life, will bring eventually an almost religious sense of the necessity for an enduring dynamism towards ever higher forms.

But these considerations belong rather to a later chapter; we are here considering simply whether one of the major defects of the present machinery of State could not be repaired by the device of introducing a new branch of the judiciary to the discovery and promotion of new men and new ideas. It is to be hoped that from such a beginning a new attitude and procedure would spread to all the multiple organs of the new society. In all the trade and commercial associations for serious people concerned with serious subjects, which it is desirable by methods already briefly described to weave into the administration of the continent of Europe, it should be possible for the suggested method of judicial procedure in the examination of new proposals gradually to replace the more haphazard and frivolous methods of present controversy. In a serious age we must finally relegate entertainment and the entertainers to the places of public amusement, and in serious matters substitute the judicial and scientific method which earnestly seeks truth as a basis for vital action.

The work of the press would naturally not be confined to entertainment, as it is so largely self-confined at present, in fact, it is to be hoped that in the new atmosphere it would emerge again to perform a part more in accord with its earlier traditions. On the other hand, if it desired simply to entertain with pictures of beautiful ladies and strip cartoons, no very strong reason indicates any interference with the liberty which some enjoy. What is far more serious, and is a threat to personal liberty, is intrusion into private life and particularly into private grief. Attacks on individuals who have no way to reply and no redress except the expensive and uncertain libel law, can also become oppressive of individual rights.

All these wrongs of the present system could be corrected by one very simple measure. Any person attacked in the press, or mentioned in the press, should have the right to equal space in reply to the attack, or in comment on the matter in which he or she had been the subject of report. If he were attacked, he could give his reply at equal length and the paper would be obliged to print it. If he were the subject of a report to which he objected, e.g. some intrusion into his private life, he would have the right to equal space in the same paper for his version of the incident and, also, for his comment on the behaviour of the journalists and press proprietors who had been responsible. His reply or comment could be as pungent as he liked, subject to the normal check of libel, and he would naturally be entitled to any expert assistance which he could secure; some very skilled pens would doubtless be at his disposal, and by no means all of them would charge any fees. Nothing would so quickly correct abuse of individual rights by the press. And it would not mean duller, but brighter newspapers; some lively comments spring to the mind which the public might make on the press lords in their own columns. The press lords, as good and disinterested journalists, would doubtless be delighted to think what fun it would provide for all.

This system of natural redress would be complete if Government, or any other corporate institution, were given the same rights as individuals. One or two of the brightest young ministers, with the appropriate expert assistance, would doubtless find themselves well occupied in replying at equal length to attacks on the government in the same newspaper. The whole method would be neatly rounded-off by a rapid procedure of injunction in the courts, if a paper refused immediately to accord the right of reply at equal length. And to compensate the press for any embarrassment occasioned, it might be relieved of some of the more onerous provisions of the libel laws, which in England, at any rate, oppress the freedom of the newspapers. Great is liberty, and the proprietors of the press should have it in ample measure; both ways.

All ideas which are novel seem fantastic, but once they have been in use for a short time they often become humdrum. In far more vital spheres than that just discussed we shall need rapidly to accustom ourselves to ideas which at first seem fantastic. After all, no suggestion to meet events is so far nearly as fantastic as the events themselves. Within the space of half a century life has become fantastic. Yet we are governed broadly by methods which were developed to deal with human affairs centuries ago, when life had few elements of fantasy beyond the normal operations of nature to which all had become accustomed. This is a development which requires a corresponding development in the method and even in the character of men. We must become less impervious to new ideas. For if we cannot match the march of science with some corresponding progress in human society, we may well be lost. The first need in the necessary training of the mind is to realise that all things are now possible. Nothing should any longer be dismissed just because it is new.

Nor should anything be discarded, just because it is traditional. On the contrary, to maintain harmony and balance in a distracting and distracted period, we need everything in our tradition that still works. For example, the British Crown should still play a most important part in the coming period; in some ways a more important part then ever. If, for instance, one of the Dominions did not at first desire, before the advantages were clearly recognised, to enter the new European economy, the Crown could still maintain the link between the Dominion and the mother country. In all other particulars the position and duty of the Crown would be unaffected; except in the one respect of the present function of the Crown on a change of government. It seems obvious that the British Crown, on the occasion of a government being defeated at an election, could not in the present sense send for new ministers, because the whole of Europe and not only Great Britain would be affected. In such a case, something like the American procedure would seem appropriate to determine the new government after a popular vote. The only difference would be that a Presidential election determines what individual shall be elected President, while in these proposals the electorate would settle which government, or team presented by a particular party, had secured its winning vote from the franchise of the European people. If a government had a four-year life as suggested, and the new government were elected by a vote of the whole European people on universal franchise at an election in which every party might enter, some such process would be necessary to give effect to the people's votes.

But in all other respects the duties of the British Crown would remain precisely what they are today. Our constitutional monarch acts on the advice of ministers; today they are British ministers, and if the British people decided to become a part of Europe they would naturally then become European ministers. The position of the other monarchs and presidents of Europe would likewise be unaffected; they could continue to perform their existing duties within the boundaries of the present countries, if so desired.

All these proposals, of course, could be changed or modified in a score of different ways without affecting any basic principles. The reader will remember that these principles in brief were: a recognition of the necessity for clear definition of function, and for a reconciliation between action by government and the maintenance of individual liberty. If these principles be accepted, the detail would still require the assistance of many expert minds for their full execution. But these pages, I hope, have at least suggested a method by which a strong executive could act as rapidly as the ever-developing modern situation required, and yet be subject to a series of checks and safeguards which would effectively preserve individual liberty. More than that, it should be possible to devise a machinery for the promotion of new ideas and new men which supplied a certain impetus and dynamism, if the requisite qualities were lacking in the executive. And beyond that, as we have seen in earlier chapters, it should be possible in a conscious conception of an organic state to use all the great resources of energy and ability in the various scientific, technical, professional, business, trade union, commercial and trading associations which today are not always fully employed in a coherent fashion in the service of the whole.

We are faced in the modern state with much complexity and much diversity. The principle of good administration must, therefore, always be to simplify and to synthesise. The first essential of simplicity is the clear definition of function, which I hope and believe the present proposals can secure. The method of a complete synthesis I suggested in a previous book under the rather clumsy name of "hierarchical synthesis". The problem to which that study was addressed seems still to persist, perhaps in an even aggravated form. Many activities of the modern State, and even many researches in the sphere of science and technics are often conducted in no relation at all to other activities and researches with which they should be closely coordinated. It is no one's fault in particular; it is due simply to the fact that the machine has become too big and the problem of the various co-relations has not been worked out. But it is essential to do it, and to do it quickly if a waste and inefficiency is not to continue, which we can now ill-afford. To that end I suggested a method of organisation in pyramid form: at the base would be all the narrowly specialised occupations, each in its separate compartment and with little relation to each other; at the next tier would be the less specialist mind which is yet capable of co-ordinating the work of a few of the specialised occupations at the base; on the next tier would be the still less specialist mind with a still wider view which had yet sufficient knowledge of the detail at the base to effect a wider co-ordination; and so on, tier upon tier, to the apex of the administrative pyramid, which in ideal form should be a general intelligence that was half statesman and half scientist; until we reach that point we must put up with a team of statesmen and scientists who understand each other well enough to get on together.

The same method with many variations and modifications might be employed in many of the different administrative machines of an organic State, which sought to use by means of the incentives of freedom all the diverse abilities the people can produce, and for their effective use to co-ordinate and to synthesise them into a coherent and purposeful whole. In short, these are principles for the entry of government into the age of science. I ask here only for acceptance of the view that we cannot travel through the epoch of the nuclear rocket in a stagecoach.

Our system of government must be brought up to date. Important in that process is the power of government to act, because we cannot live without action in a period of such great and fast-moving events. But human freedom and the good life can certainly be reconciled with action by government; in fact, not only happiness but life itself can now depend on timely and wise action by government.

Chapter 6

European Socialism

The Wage Price Mechanism

IF we can do everything we want in a simple way, it is a mistake to complicate it. If we can solve our problems in Europe-Africa by means of the economic leadership of Government, simply operating the wage-price mechanism, it can be an error to carry thought from the previous period of poverty economics into a new age of plenty economics. For instance, the ownership of industry becomes almost irrelevant when a government elected by the people can hold the balance between wage, profit and investment by means of a regular machinery, and can thus lead and guide the European economy in the direction required by the interests of the whole. Why then bother with changes in the structure of industry? And why should the workers bother with its detailed conduct? If they can be sure of a fair share in a continually expanding production, will they any longer be interested in questions of ownership? Could not the successful operation of the wage-price mechanism make much former economic thinking irrelevant; including mine?

These questions arise inevitably if a method so simple in principle, and far-reaching in effect, as the wage-price mechanism be valid. We should never complicate anything just for the sake of complication. And let us remember always that first thinking tends to be complicated but later thinking becomes relatively simple. It seems that the wage-price mechanism can secure everything desired by the system of thinking which I described as European socialism, except in two respects; and the question will arise whether either of them in the new circumstances will be necessary.

Europe: Faith and Plan

I first used the phrase European Socialism on May Day, 1950, in a speech, in East London. Some years later, after a discussion of the principles involved in several countries I reduced the definition of the subject to the following brief description:

"European Socialism is the development by a fully united Europe of all the resources in our own continent, in white Africa, and in South America, for the benefit of all the peoples of Europe and of these other European lands, with every energy and incentive that the action of European government can give to private enterprise, workers' ownership or any other method of progress which science and a dynamic system of government find most effective for the enrichment of all our people and the lifting of European civilisation to ever higher forms of life."

It now seems clear to me that these objectives can very well be secured within the viable area of Europe-Africa by the economic leadership of government using no other means than the wage-price mechanism. This can secure all the objectives involved, except two, the syndicalist principle in certain industries and a fundamental change in the method of taxation. Let us now examine these two points and consider the extent to which they may, or may not, be necessary in the new system.

At once, I state a preference for the conduct and development of industries already nationalised by syndicalist method rather than by the present state bureaucracy. It is far healthier for industries which have already lost the principle of private enterprise to be owned and conducted by the workers in them than by the mandarins of state socialism. Either method would, of course, under our system be subject to the wage-price mechanism. The wages of these industries would also be determined by government, and, as they are monopolies, the prices they charged would be determined by government. In these conditions it would surely be far better that they should be worker-owned, and that the workers in them should be told they would get the benefit of any increased efficiency, which kept the prices they charged stable but enabled their own wages to be raised. Such direct incentive to efficiency and workers' co-operation in new methods would bring far better results than leaving the matter to the present functionaries who have no direct personal interest in efficiency, or even much concern whether the industry runs at profit or loss.

In this way could operate the collective individualism which is the supreme merit of syndicalism because it restores the incentive which bureaucratic socialism destroys. But the further question arises whether other industries should be syndicalised as they became what is now termed ripe for nationalisation. The basic idea of European Socialism in this respect was that industries should become worker-owned instead of nationalised at the point when the original individual initiative was entirely lost, and they became large, long-established concerns which were in effect conducted by a bureaucracy, and often also acquired a monopoly character.

European socialism envisaged a natural development of industry in due chronological order. Worthwhile new things nearly always come from the initiative of the individual, in economic matters from an industrial pioneer. This man is the mainspring of any effective system and of all progress; he should in all conditions above all be encouraged and cherished. But at the point when he dies, or becomes old and retires, industry should not pass to the control of a bureaucrat employed by the state, but should be owned by the workers who have been the comrades of the industrial pioneer and are therefore his natural heirs and successors. The founder of a business should draw his full reward and so should his family - who could always conduct the business as long as they were able to do it - but when the original character of the concern was entirely lost, and it became too big for any individual management, it should be the workers and not the state-paid mandarins who then conducted it. Such, in a very brief survey, was the industrial structure suggested in the system of thinking which I described as European socialism.

It was a synthesis between private enterprise and socialism, using each motive force at the appropriate period of industrial development. That private enterprise was to be in every sense a freer private enterprise than it is today - as always in our thinking - while the socialism derived from the syndicalist and not from the bureaucratic tradition of European thinking. The turning point toward disaster in previous socialist thinking seemed to us always the rejection of guild socialism in favour of state socialism; the natural movement of the workers then gave way to bureaucracy, and the "inevitability of gradualism"; in short, to the rule of the mandarin which has persisted ever since in the theory and practice of the British Labour Party, and of other socialist parties in the second international. This system of thinking, like Marxism itself - which was more thoroughly understood on the Continent - was essentially oriental in inspiration, and the opposite in every way to the live tradition of the true European movement which began in the Guilds of the great cities in England and Germany during the middle ages, and later found vigorous expression in France, Italy, and elsewhere as the syndicalist movement. State socialism brought the dead hand of the remote functionary, the bureaucrat, the mandarin, the Chinese idol behind a Whitehall desk, which slowly stifled the vitality from the live body of the natural and organic movement of the English and European workers.

We sought to bring back the true tradition of the working-class movement and at the same time to find a synthesis with the indispensable force of private enterprise and individual initiative at a higher level, where the driving impulses of both systems exercised in due time and on due occasion, could give forward and harmonious urge to the whole. This attempt in new thinking was right and necessary, but it may well now be surpassed by further thinking and by greater possibilities. The plain fact, which must be recognised by all realists, is that the workers have very little interest in questions of the ownership of industry, or any other theoretical matters, when things are going really well. Small blame to them, for they find better things to do with their spare time and money than attending committee meetings; and as opportunity occurs for real leisure, holidays, travel, and general culture arising from protracted facilities of education, the use of spare time and money will find ever more desirable outlets.

If we can construct the economy of Europe-Africa and then release within it the force of modern science, both to increase wealth production and to reduce the hours of labour, the thoughts of the workers are likely to turn increasingly to higher things than the old industrial dogfight which found expression in acute questions of the ownership of industry. And this will not necessarily mean a lessening of social consciousness, but rather an extension and deepening of individual consciousness. Already the tendency is notable whenever for a short time things go well; it is bound to gather force and momentum directly an economic system which is both stable and expanding brings durable hopes of a fuller life for the mass of the people.

In short, if we resolve the main economic problem through the wage-price mechanism, syndicalism tomorrow may look as irrelevant as nationalisation begins to look today. Very few of the workers may want to be bothered at all with such things. But the people who will continue very much to be bothered with the daily life and development of the great concerns which they administer, will be the new class of managers and industrial technicians. For the next stage of development we may have to look more to the managerial revolution than to syndicalism. When the individual pioneer and his family pass away and the concern becomes too big for any form of individual management, it is the new category of highly trained managers and departmental experts who are ready to take over. Not only does their life depend on the business, but their life is in the business. They are a new and most desirable phenomenon; they should be encouraged and cherished by the industrial system as much as the original pioneer to whose first impulse all subsequent developments are due.

Again, the system of differential rewards must enter decisively and seriously. These men are worth a lot, and they must get it. They must be paid more and taxed less. A considerable share of the larger amount of distributable wealth - which will come from scientific development, automation, and mass production for a large and completely assured market - must go to them; they must rank next to the scientists for the first cut at the bigger cake.

The new managers must be brought forward to play an ever more conscious role. They must above all develop the leadership capacity which we envisaged for the managers under syndicalism. Even generals in the field today have to lead and to persuade as well as to command. Modern command is persuasion. The day of the remote industrial tycoon is over. The modern industrial leaders must really be able to lead; they must have personality as well as knowledge, charm as well as drive. Naturally, not all managers will perform the same part; the division of function is clearly necessary in proportion to the size of the concern. But in principle the figure of chief manager must cease to be the figure of the boss and become the figure of the leader. He will be the captain of a team and not its driver. At the point when the role of the new managers becomes decisive, the industrial future may well rest between them and the Trade Union leadership which increasing opportunity will evoke.

Government, in exercising economic leadership through the wage-price mechanism, as already noted, must seek not only the co-operation of European Trade Unionism but must be ready to devolve upon it as an "estate of the realm" many of the duties of the state. Trade Unionism, for instance, should be asked to deal with all questions affecting conditions of work, unemployment pay, welfare, sick pay, holidays, compensation claims, legal representation. The administration of these matters should be entirely taken over by the Trades Unions. This can be one of the ways in which the new system will avoid the development of bureaucracy. To this end we must rely very largely on existing trades unions and employers' organisations to perform many vital services to industry.

So far from a new system requiring a bigger bureaucracy, it will be possible considerably to dismantle the present bureaucratic apparatus when we enter a larger and healthier life. When it is possible for all men to live well, it will not be necessary to support them in living badly. The unhealthy body requires every kind of support, ranging from stays for holding it upright to iron lungs. But the healthy body can support itself, and live better for so doing. We must get away from the whole system of charity, national and international, and develop self-help within a system of endless opportunity.

All social services should be made contributory, with consequent saving both to the state and individual. The economy to the state is obvious, but the individual can also gain by not paying for benefits he does not require and by directing his own contributions to the services he wants. The state will save an expensive bureaucracy necessary to maintain the present system, and the individual will no longer be made to pay for what he does not want.

Fear is the basis of the present system, fear of all the manifold mischances of a system of chaos. Once we enter a stable system of unlimited opportunities for all, men and women will be glad to ensure themselves only against the misfortunes they apprehend, and to avoid paying for a great paraphernalia of compulsory solicitude in which they have not the slightest interest. Self-help must be the basis of a healthy future, combined with every chance for economical insurance against life's misfortunes such as accident, illness, death or anything else which the individual may freely choose to guard against.

All the other expensive props of the feeble structure of the modern state will be rendered unnecessary by the policy already described. Agriculture, for instance, will need no subsidies when it is clearly recognised that primary producers must be paid more, and that a good proportion of the increased production for the larger and assured market of Europe-Africa must be set aside for the purpose. No man and no industry need live on charity, when all can earn more in a life of larger opportunity than present limitations permit. When we plunge into the water of that greater life, let us begin by washing ourselves clean of all the slime of subsidy and charity with which the body economic is enfeebled today.

Let us, also, in all things relate reward directly to effort. Already the introduction of a really decisive system of differential reward has been discussed, which will encourage all both to acquire skill and to accept responsibility. Incentive can be extended with piecework in every form, not merely of the individual, but also of the team. Reward, either individual or collective, should be directly related to effort. All these strong motive forces have been largely inhibited in the modern state by fear of unemployment, by the well-founded apprehension that any higher rate of production in whole or in particular will lead to indisposable surplus and consequent break-down of the system. But once operation of the wage-price mechanism has begun, clearly and successfully, to equate production and consumption, the fear of surplus, breakdown and unemployment will vanish. All the restrictive practices of today, which arise from old fears with real foundations in the present system, will be swept away by the urge to produce and earn, once it is proved that production means fairly distributed wealth and not another collapse into unemployment and poverty.

Nearly all the evils of the present industrial system arise from fear, and that fear in turn arises from the chaos of a system which must buy and sell on international markets in conditions increasingly impossible for the European governments. The firm grip of the wage-price mechanism within a viable area which possesses its own supply and its own market, can assure every worker that his increased effort will have no other effect than his increased reward. The whole psychology of industry will change once the new system wins confidence because its operation is observed.

The incentive of reward should be accompanied by an incentive to save. As every Bonapartist soldier carried in his knapsack the Marshall's baton, so should everyone who works in any way in the new Europe carry with him the possibility of founding a great industry or of rising in some other way to its summit. Already certain means have been suggested by which the inventor and the industrial pioneer can be assisted by finance which carries through a new process from the crude experiment to the open market. But, in addition, far greater opportunities should be open to the individual to save and to finance himself. The present burden of taxation in many countries puts this possibility out of the question. A man could not start with a small bicycle shop today and save enough at each stage from his own profits to build the greatest automobile industry in the country. We must restore the situation in which men of energy and talent could lift themselves to the top without help from anyone.

The general level of taxation will, of course, be automatically reduced by a greater output of wealth through mass production for a large and assured market; a lesser tax on a greater turnover can yield the same return. In addition, the pooling of overheads in a united Europe in every sphere of national life will provide immense economies, quite apart from special measures we have considered to reduce bureaucracy and create a healthier system. We can be stronger and better organised in every sphere at less expense; all the economies of a great merger will be present in addition to increased output and profit from an enlarged market. So the crippling burden of present taxation will naturally be lifted by entering into a larger system, and the creative individual will receive proportionate relief from a load which today crushes him and inhibits new enterprise.

But should we not go further with means to encourage saving and to enable men from their own savings to build new industries?

Should not taxation be largely shifted from income to expenditure, and become a tax on what a man spends and not on what he earns? At present various devices for expenditure tax as such, have considerable attraction. They have stood up to severe test, for one such system was apparently approved by the American Treasury in the war but never subsequently applied. But the main difficulty about expenditure tax is that it hits directly the man we most desire to encourage, the man who by our standards is most worthy. The scientist, the inventor, who is also an entrepreneur, and sells on the market at fairly regular intervals the product of his brains, may choose to spend the proceeds and to do it in a big way if his creations are worth much. And why shouldn't he? If any man has a right to a big reward, it is this type.

Why should he not spend the reward, and live very well if he wishes? If we discourage such men, we are drying up the very spring of progress. Everything about them is what we want to encourage. They create, they enrich the community as well as themselves; they even spend as they go, instead of trying to accumulate some system of hereditary usury which, if it goes too far, can distort the whole economy. They are in every way admirable people; yet they might be hit and frustrated by an expenditure tax. Therefore they would have to be exempted, and with them the whole large and worthy host of men who build businesses which they subsequently sell with a desire to spend the proceeds. They range from the scientific entrepreneur to the farmer and the shopkeeper. It is true that, if they have saved, they keep what they have earned under the system of expenditure tax. But it is not freedom to compel a man to save, and within an economy of this kind which was really working, compulsory saving might very quickly become over-saving.

All such men would in any case have to be exempted from an expenditure tax. This fiscal weapon must not shoot them in a general broadside, which is primarily aimed at the guinea-pig director with a fake expense account. This phenomenon, which is rotting the present fiscal system, derives from a general system which is dying, in fact decomposing. The level of taxation is so intolerably high in the effort to support national burdens which are insupportable for the small divided nations, that individuals will go to any length to avoid the burden of tax which in turn is insupportable to them. That problem will no longer arise when the general level of taxation is lower within the larger system for reasons already given. When the general health is fully restored it will no longer be necessary to fake the fever chart.

Thus, expenditure tax, which we have sometimes contemplated as a necessary expedient in Great Britain, is likely to be unnecessary in the larger and freer system here recommended. In any case the proposal for expenditure tax will have to be altered out of all recognition to free from its operation men who create things most valuable to the country, and thereby rightly earn a large reward, and have a most natural desire to enjoy it.

What could be done most effectively, however, is to shift a large part of the burden from direct to indirect taxation in order to assist the saver and let the spender pay. In this region again we are faced with a legacy of fear from the epoch of poverty economics. Such proposals were often designed to make the poor carry the burden and let off the rich. On the contrary, I would propose that every necessity of life be entirely free from tax; all the basic necessities which today are often heavily taxed. Then a graduated luxury tax should be introduced, which would increase in severity as the article passed from any possible sphere of utility or necessity into the category of pure luxury. Naturally the definition of a luxury would change and become ever more liberal as the standard of life rose. Something which is a luxury in the siege-economy of a beleaguered island (which Britain may become by persisting in present policies) can be regarded as a near necessity in the standard of life which will be natural in an expanding continental economy.

But in that case the whole burden of taxation would be relieved as total output increased, and a lower tax secured a greater revenue. When the standard of life in the new system rises, the problem of taxation will progressively diminish. But as we pass from poverty to plenty economics, we should not miss the opportunity to encourage the saver and the doer at the expense of the spendthrift and profligate. It is wrong that a man who saves every penny in order to build his own business should be taxed in the same way as the man who just wants to throw his money about; but that is the effect of direct taxation, particularly at a very high level. Let us set the doers free, and use the fiscal system also to that end.

Every incentive should encourage the natural tendency of most men and women who work to make money for themselves and their family, in order to obtain the things which money can buy. There is an elite of mankind to be found in every section of life, which works as the creative artist works, for the joy of work and creation in itself. Others work for honour and recognition by their fellows rather than for reward. But the great majority work quite simply to make money for themselves and their families, and any sensible system must be organised to satisfy this most honourable desire in work which also serves the whole community, by relating reward to effort.

The interest of family in many cases is a stronger factor than personal interest. That is why we must tread carefully in dealing with the impulse which heredity gives to the whole social system. It is true that great accumulations of hereditary wealth tend to deform the whole body economic with a wasteful and lopsided form of demand, but the desire to accumulate wealth for their families after their own death is the urge which keeps many of the creative people working, and making new enterprises long after they would otherwise have ceased to exert themselves. It is true also that a hereditary class whose members may themselves have contributed nothing to the good of the community, tends to undermine the best social values of duty and service; yet the desire to give his children a better start in life is one of the motives which inspire many who contribute most to those values.

It is, also, surely clear that a farmer who bequeathed his farm to his son, or a man who leaves a family business to his family, should be able to do so without the family continuance of the business being stopped by death duties. In such concerns the hereditary principle in work and service is as desirable as the creation of a hereditary burden is undesirable.

In this difficult sphere of contradictory national interests, we have already in these pages noted that once again the wage-price mechanism can deal effectively with yet another evil of the day. It will be impossible to accumulate such great wealth through profit and to transmit it to descendants (at the expense of the purchasing power of the mass of the people, who provide the general market) that demand becomes distorted in undesirable directions to an extent which jeopardises the whole economy. Long before any such event occurred, the wage-price mechanism in responsible and capable hands would have pushed up wages at the expense of profit to check any such dangerous tendencies. A government exercising economic leadership by these means would be able immediately to correct any development of the kind before it became dangerous, as a skilful driver corrects a skid.

But in addition to these inherent safeguards of an organised and consciously directed system, a scientific method of death duties could, if necessary, be devised both to preserve incentive for a creative individual to the end of his days, and yet to prevent great accumulations of invested wealth being handed down from one generation to another as a charge on those who work and create. Here again it should be emphasised that, when we pass from the present system of poverty economics in a small island to the system of plenty economics in two continents, it is improbable that we shall require any such system of severe death duties. But it is worth mentioning this subject in brief to show how easy it is with new methods like the wage-price mechanism to meet the old Marxian dilemmas of the Left. We can answer all the Marxian arguments with the wage-price mechanism alone, if we strip them of their jargon and reduce them to their practical application, but a little ingenuity can, also, easily fashion other devices to reinforce that answer, if it were ever necessary.

In fact, Marx observed certain natural laws of the capitalist economy in its very early stages, which will operate if nothing is done to check or to alter them. In the same way Newton observed a natural law which in practical application meant a man would break his neck if he jumped over a high cliff with nothing to support him. Later men invented the balloon, the parachute, the aeroplane and finally the rocket to suspend the operation of that natural law and to enable men to defy its consequences. In the same way there are many effective ways of preventing the fatal operation of the Marxian laws, without adopting the rigid and brutal despotism of communism. I believe the economic leadership of government by means of the wage-price mechanism can provide a complete answer to Marx at every point, and I am always ready to sustain that contention in public debate.

If, in conclusion of this subject, I may be permitted an element of fantasy by present standards, a truly civilised community might give a number of gifted people the means to show how beautiful life could be; a process which is exactly the opposite to the present system of giving a number of ungifted people the means to show how silly life can be. Once we have solved the basic problem of providing the means to live well, by organising a market for the new production of which science is capable - a market which will simply be the fair reward of all who work according to their effort, assured by a conscious, deliberate and organised mechanism of the state - we can use some portion of future increases in production as a surplus, which may legitimately be used for elevating our way of life and enhancing the beauty of human existence. We must always put first things first, and the first charge on any surplus must certainly be the pure research of science which is responsible for most of the extraordinary advance of humanity, but we should also use some of the new resources for purposes which make life worth living when that progress has been achieved.

Chapter 7

The Party

THE party can be the greatest influence in the modern world, for good or evil. The organised political party - or movement as it is usually called, when it represents an idea which is fundamental, and a party method which is serious - can be a greater influence in the state than even the Press, radio, television, cinema or any other of the multiple instruments of the established interest and the money power. This has always been the case in relatively modern times. The party must, of course, represent a clear and decisive idea of the period, an idea which the people want because its time has come. The party must also have a real national organisation, which should aim at covering every street and village in the country. Then the party is paramount.

This rule does not apply, of course, if the party is merely a social organisation, which supplies a few voluntary workers at an election, and is kept together in between elections just by social occasions interspersed with a few polite lectures on matters of current interest. To be effective in this decisive sense the party must be a party of men and women dedicated to an idea, which continually functions in promotion of that idea; a real political movement is more akin to a religious order than a social organisation.

Such a concept of the party has been discarded in very recent times, together with many other good things which were thrown away wholesale with some bad things. But an influence so great as that of a real party is bound to return with serious times, when serious ideas and serious people are again in demand. It is well, therefore, to consider what is good and what is bad in the character of such a movement; experience can now surely help us to preserve the good and discard the bad.

The first question, again, is how to reconcile the dynamic element in the state - which can be such a party - with the complete maintenance in every way of individual liberty, which is essential. Not to maintain liberty coincidentally with the party, is fatal to the state and quite as disastrous to the party. That is why, despite some advantages in securing rapid action in time of stress and danger, any idea which approaches the totalitarian party must be discarded. This is done by ensuring that in the election of a government, held every four years in these proposals, any party may enter in conditions which are entirely free for all. A party cannot then become totalitarian, except by a coup d'état to set aside the constitution, which is ruled out in modern conditions, as everyone must know who has given any serious attention to the history of the subject. It is eliminated because any political party is quite helpless in an appeal to force against modern weapons; a coup d'état by a political party belongs to the days of the street barricades, and not to the period of such weapons as nuclear rockets.

A coup d'état could only be attempted today by a force in possession of the decisive weapons; namely the armed forces. And as we have seen in many examples of the last forty years, regular military forces are quite impotent in any advanced country to impose a coup d'état in face of the resistance of the workers and of the civilian population in general. Even a combination between such a political party and the armed forces would be quite unable to assume power against the wishes of the mass of the people, because life in an advanced state simply comes to a standstill if the people do not go to work. Armies and parties can march in, even together, but they just have to march out again if the people do not want them. Many examples render this indisputable in the modern world. Force only succeeds with the full brutality of soviet terror, as in Hungary; even then, only when world opinion was diverted, by British Government's intervention at Suez.

Therefore all chances of any political party becoming totalitarian are excluded, if the state be governed by a constitutional

The Party

enactment that all elections are free to all parties. A party cannot then remain indefinitely in power by suppressing all its rivals. It must accept the fact that it can only rule by persuasion; and it must accept the further fact of defeat, when this occurs. And, strangely enough, acceptance of this fact of electoral defeat is as good for the party as it is for the state; in the light of experience, it is quite essential to the well being of the party. Human nature being what it is, parties which remain indefinitely in power, and are secure against defeat, produce inevitably many people who are quite insufferable.

The old axiom, that "all power corrupts", has doubtful validity, because it derives from our neglect of Plato's advice to find men carefully and train them by methods which make them fit for power. But if it be true in any degree, that power corrupts great men, how much truer must it be that power corrupts small men? This is precisely why we can never leave too much power in the hands of a multiplicity of little party officials or even of civil servants. And a party which is totalitarian, in the sense that it enjoys absolute and indefinite power, inevitably produces in many localities and in diverse regions of the national life a host of little functionaries whose heads are turned by power, and who will consequently become intolerable.

Among them, of course, and in any real and true movement far exceeding them in number, are a larger host of dedicated men and women who preserve their sense of service in victory and defeat, who are there not to command but to help, not to dominate with authority but to lead with example. And the supreme merit of defeat to a great party is that it purges the worst and preserves the best; not sweet, but vital, are the uses of political adversity. A great party returns from a severe defeat, stronger and purer; better fitted for a high mission. In the light of all our experience, any man who values and loves such a movement should not desire its perpetual power. Let it accept defeat; the truth within it will ensure that it comes again.

A real party with a creed which is not ephemeral but organic, a movement which is a continuing and developing influence within the nation as the nation itself continues and develops, can afford to accept defeat. It can tolerate the temporary triumph of rivals with different character, parties which are constructed in another way and for different, lighter purposes. The true movement of the people will always return in due course, and will be the permanent, functioning influence in the life of the nation. Such a party beside the parties of today can be reality beside the shadows; their existence would not trouble it for a moment. And if it be not the true movement it is right that it should accept eclipse, for another answer must be found. The true party can accept the test of time.

Once Europe is made, time will no longer press so much. So many of the faults of the past arose from time pressure; and it was right to have that sense, for in the old, small individual nations we live in perpetual crises, and will so live until these nations pass into Europe. A party which experiences defeat in these conditions can feel that everything which matters, the life, history, the very being of a great nation may be obliterated before it can return again to its task. Such a sense of urgency was the reason for many things which have been condemned, and which were wrong. But once Europe is made, time should no longer press in the same way. If we obtain peace, at best by disarmament, and at worst by the paralysis of force, the present dread of extinction from external menace will be lifted. If we resolve the more pressing economic problems in a large and viable area by measures already described, we shall pass from the epoch of poverty to the age of plenty economics. Time does not press so hard in conditions of peace and plenty. The character even of that continuing and persisting dynamism which is essential to all human advance, can change and can modify its methods when time no longer presses. In peace and plenty all will have time to think and to persuade.

What, then, should be the character and method of such a party in the new Europe; a party which seeks a mandate from the vote of the people for very definite purposes whenever that confidence is accorded? The character of the party should be suited to a movement of dedicated men and women, given to a purpose which moves their whole lives. The character should be more that of a church than that of a political party, though its work for reasons we will consider in the next chapter will never contradict or traverse the work of the existing churches. But it will be animated by a sense of service and of dedication, and this will make it in character more akin to a church. And it should be organised more in the way of a church than in the way of any existing political party.

No one can claim that any suitable rules for the organisation of such a party are an infringement of liberty, because anyone under the free constitution proposed can leave the party any day he wishes. On the other hand a man cannot easily leave the nation to which he belongs, and his utmost freedom and liberty of action have to be preserved by law if the whole principle of liberty is not to be brought into jeopardy. But it is idle to say that a man's liberty is affected by the rules of any society which he joins as a voluntary member, and which he can leave when he likes. On the contrary, if in the name of liberty the members of a party are prevented from organising themselves in the way they desire, their liberty to live as they wish is impaired. It is superfluous to add that this does not imply liberty to organise for the overthrow of the state, or for any such purpose of violence and subversion. But, subject to these elementary provisions of law and order, a party should be free to devise rules which make it a disciplined, and therefore an effective party. It should be organised like a church in a hierarchy of authority, which can oppress no one because any man is free to leave it any day he wishes.

The party which really serves the people and is, therefore, organised to that end, should be represented by a single, responsible individual in every street of the great cities and in every village of the countryside. That person should be there to serve the people, to help them in need, to assist and to advise.

Someone should always be there representing the party to whom anyone can turn in time of trouble, and not only in time of trouble but in any matter of everyday life which needs the helping hand. And anything the individual worker could not do, should be done by referring to the party worker at the next level who would be responsible for aiding several of the workers we have just discussed, and who would if necessary refer it through the hierarchy of organisation until the whole influence of the party was mobilised to assist whoever was in trouble or in need of help. Such a party would be a movement of continually available service to the people; it would be of the people and with the people, and interwoven with their daily life.

Within its ranks the barriers of social class would be unknown. They are, in any case, an anachronism and an absurdity in the modern state. An age in which great scientists work with their hands, and most manual workers have to use their heads in high degree, will soon make this plain even to the last surviving victim of nineteenth century political indoctrination. To feel class in any sense is already a sure sign of inadequacy to this period; the fact of feeling it establishes a man's intellectual and spiritual inferiority, whether he was born in a castle or a slum. The better minds and characters simply do not know any longer what such sentiments mean. The only question with a fellow man is whether he is of like mind and spirit. It is the duty of the party to bring that attitude to every street and village in the country, where archaic sentiments of class may still linger.

The influence of such a party would naturally be very great, but nobody could possibly believe it was an oppressive influence. Any individual in any street could tell a party worker he never wanted to see him again, and the whole electorate could convey the same sharp message to the Party as a whole at an election. And the attitude of the individual in the street would be the same as the position of the party as a whole in electoral adversity: a willingness to retire temporarily in a period of national fatigue, but a certainty of return in the moment of need and action.

The Party

A party should be a movement of service, but also of leadership; a companion to the people, ever at hand to help, but also a leader on paths which lead upward to new and unproven heights. It should be the duty of a party to look ahead, think ahead, feel ahead, live ahead. For such ends it will need its general staff of thinkers and planners, of visionaries too; men and women at home in every sphere of contemporary thought and feeling, from the laboratories of science to the regions of pure thought and imagination, of literature, philosophy, poetry and art. Such a movement should seek always to be in the vanguard of the human march, a leader in all adventures of the mind and spirit.

Should the way of life, also, approach the method of a religious or monastic order? I would answer definitely, no. The party should always not only be in touch with the world, but at one with all things human, and with nature itself. At this point we approach moral questions which some may feel are outside the range of politics, and certainly we have no right on questions of personal life to seek in any way to impose our views on others. Every man's outlook on such matters is his private affair, and entirely different principles in such things should and could in no way impede political co-operation. But for purposes of a political party it should not be impossible to state a minimum on which all could agree. I would suggest only two essential principles. The first is that in all things we should keep our word, whether to friend or foe. The word of honour is sacred; that is the very basis of European values. No advantage can justify the breaking of this principle, and if it be gained by the loss of the principle it is not even an advantage. Nothing pays man or movement so well as for everyone to know that their word is sacred to them.

Communism has been terribly injured by the doctrine that any lie, trick or breach of word is justified if used against the enemy. This teaching rotted their own movement, because they had only to regard a fellow communist as an enemy in order to justify all the horrors which have occurred in Russia; the murder of a party comrade or his frame up for judicial murder in the notorious trials was the logical end of all that. Once honour in dealing with all men, and complete loyalty to each other are set aside, the end is not only an abyss of horror but of chaos and final disintegration. No one can trust anyone when the root values of honour are gone. And when trust exists nowhere in the world, human life in this complex society is unlikely long to continue. Therefore, the first rule must be that our word to any man must be held, whatever the cost.

The second simple principle of party morality which I would suggest, is that no one should do anything which hurt himself - which physically or mentally impaired his capacity to serve and to give his best - and that no one should do anything which hurt others, which injured his companions in life. That surely is all the morality which a party can require; it is the whole morality. For the rest we should seek to be at one with nature rather than against the creative force of the world. We should have within us the joy of life fulfilment and not the frustration of life denial. A movement of history and destiny should be a guardian and companion of the vital nature spirit in a persisting dynamism towards higher forms. For those who think that such ideals are too fanciful and exalted for a political party, we may reply that we shall remain in the mud until we can lift our eyes beyond it.

Chapter 8

The Doctrine of Higher Forms

WHAT then, is the purpose of it all? Is it just material achievement? Will the whole urge be satisfied when everyone has plenty to eat and drink, every possible assurance against sickness and old age, a house, a television set and a long seaside holiday each year? What other end, for example, can communist civilisation hold in prospect except this, which modern science can so easily satisfy in the next few years? If you begin with the belief that all history can be interpreted only in material terms, and that any spiritual purpose is a trick and a delusion, which has the simple object of distracting the workers from the material aim of improving their conditions - the only reality - what end can there be even after every conceivable success, except the satisfaction of further material desires? When all the basic needs and wants are sated by the output of the new science, what further aim can there be but the devising of ever more fantastic amusements to titillate material appetites? If soviet civilisation achieves its furthest ambitions, is the end to be sputnik races round the stars to relieve the tedium of being a communist?

Communism is a limited creed, and its limitations are inevitable. If the original impulse is envy, malice, and hatred against someone who has something you have not got, you are inevitably limited by the whole impulse to which you owe the origin of your faith and movement. That initial emotion may be very well founded, may be based on justice, on indignation against the vile treatment of the workers in the early days of the industrial revolution. But if you hold that creed, you carry within yourself your own prison walls, because any escape from that origin seems to lead towards the hated shape of the man who once had something you had not got; anything above or beyond yourself is bad. In reality, he may be very far from being a higher form; he may, in fact, be a most decadent product of an easy living which he was incapable of using even for self-development, an ignoble example of missed opportunity. But if the whole first impulse be envy and hatred of him, you are inhibited from any movement beyond yourself for fear of becoming like him, the man who had something which you had not got.

Thus your ideal becomes not something beyond yourself, still less beyond anything which now exists, but rather, the petrified, fossilised shape of that section of the community which was most oppressed, suffering and limited by every material circumstance in the middle of the nineteenth century. The real urge is then to drag everything down toward the lowest level of life, rather than to attempt to raise everything towards the highest level of life which has yet been attained, and finally to move far beyond even that. In all things this system of values seeks what is low instead of what is high.

So communism has no longer any deep appeal to the sane, sensible mass of the European workers who, in entire contradiction of Marxian belief in their increasing immiseration, have moved by the effort of their own trade unions and by political action to at least a partial participation in the plenty which the new science is beginning to bring, and towards a way of living and an outlook in which they do not recognise themselves at all as the miserable and oppressed figure of communism's original worker. On the contrary, they know very well that they have got far beyond this, and they have knowledge enough of modern life's possibilities to be quite determined to give the children they love a better chance than they had, and an opportunity to move as far beyond them as they have moved beyond their grandfathers.

The ideal is no longer the martyred form of the oppressed, but the beginning of a higher form. Men are beginning not to look down, but to look up. And it is precisely at this point that a new way of political thinking can give definite shape to what many are beginning to feel is a new forward urge of humanity. It becomes an impulse of nature itself directly man is free from the stifling oppression of dire, primitive need.

The ideal of creating a higher form on earth can now rise before men with the power of a spiritual purpose, which is not simply a philosophic abstraction but a concrete expression of a deep human desire. All men want their children to live better than they have lived, just as they have tried by their own exertions to lift themselves beyond the level of their fathers whose affection and sacrifice often gave them the chance to do it. This is a right and natural urge in mankind, and, when fully understood, becomes a spiritual purpose. It is the way the world works, has always worked from the most primitive beginnings to the relative heights where humanity stands today. And we may, therefore, believe that if there be divine purpose, this is how it is expressed in practical life.

To state this as a political belief, is in no way to traverse the position or work of the churches. This is the last thing any man would wish to do who seeks to combat the all-prevailing materialism of the age. On the contrary, he must desire to sustain rather than to undermine the work of the churches. And it is surely clear that a belief cannot challenge the position of the churches if it can be held by someone who belongs to any church, or to none.

To believe that the purpose of life is a movement from lower to higher forms is to record an observable fact. If we reject that fact, we reject every finding of modern science, as well as the evidence of our own eyes. A man may hold this belief who does not accept the tenets of any religion, who denies the whole concept of a deity. Or a man may hold it and at the same time believe, as I do, that it is improbable something so complex as the universe assembled itself under such elaborate laws by chance, or that the long process of evolution was determined by nothing more than a series of accidents. It is necessary to believe that this is the purpose of life, because we can observe that this is the way the world works, whether we believe in divine purpose or not. And once we believe this is the way the world works, and deduce from the long record that it is the only way it can work, this becomes for us a purpose because it is the only means by which the world is likely to work in future. If the purpose fails, the world fails.

The purpose so far has achieved the most incredible results - incredible to anyone who had been told in advance what was going to happen - by working from the most primitive life forms to the relative heights of the present human form. Purpose becomes, therefore, quite clearly in the light of modern knowledge a movement from lower to higher forms. And if purpose in this way has moved so far and achieved so much, it is only reasonable to assume that it will so continue if it continues at all; if the world lasts. Therefore, if we desire to sustain human existence, if we believe in mankind's origin which science now makes clear, and in his destiny which a continuance of the same process makes possible, we must desire to aid rather than to impede the discernible purpose. That means we should serve the purpose which moves from lower to higher forms; this becomes our creed of life. Our life is dedicated to the purpose.

In practical terms this surely indicates that we should not tell men to be content with themselves as they are, but should urge them to strive to become something beyond themselves. Those who wish men to reach higher, have sometimes been accused of arrogance on account of this desire. Yet surely not to be completely content with yourself is not arrogance, but rather the reverse. On the other hand, to assure men that we have no need to surpass ourselves, and thereby to imply that men are perfect, is surely the extreme of arrogant presumption. It is also a most dangerous folly, because it is rapidly becoming clear that if mankind's moral nature and spiritual stature cannot increase more commensurately with his material achievements, we risk the death of the world owing to the sheer inadequacy of man to use properly the means of life he now possesses. We must get away from this worship of man as he is.

It is essential to improve ourselves as well as the material conditions of the world. We must learn to live, as well as to do. We must restore harmony with life, and recognise the purpose in life. Man has released the forces of nature, just as he has become separated from nature; this is a mortal danger and is reflected in the neurosis of the age. We cannot stay just where we are; it is an uneasy, perilous and impossible situation. Man must either reach beyond his present self, or fail; and if he fails this time, the failure is final. That is the basic difference between this age and all previous periods. It was never before possible for the failure of men to bring the world to an end.

It is not only a reasonable aim to strive for a higher form among men; it is a creed with the strength of a religious conviction. It is not only a plain necessity of the new age of science which the genius of man's mind has brought; it is in accordance with the long process of nature within which we may read the purpose of the world. And it is no small and selfish aim, for we work not only for ourselves but for a time to come. The long striving of our lives can not only save our present civilisation, but can also enable others more fully to realise and to enjoy the great beauty of this world, not only in peace and happiness, but in an ever unfolding wisdom and rising consciousness of the mission of man.